Depression

This book serves as a practical and comprehensive introduction to depression and its deep roots in trauma.

Marianne Leuzinger-Bohleber looks at the heterogeneous and complex phenomenon of depression and considers a range of topics essential to those faced with the challenge posed by the illness. Throughout the chapters, Leuzinger-Bohleber looks at the central experience of powerlessness and helplessness, the impact of trauma and transgenerational transmission, as well as clinical research and medical intervention. Throughout, she reviews and explains up-to-date clinical research findings and guides the reader on how to apply these in a clinical setting across a wide range of aspects within the psychodynamic understanding of depression.

Including a review of both classical psychoanalytic texts and state-of-the-art empirical research, this introductory book is an invaluable resource for psychoanalysts and psychotherapists in private practice and Public Health institutions alike. The clear and accessible style also makes it a vital resource for students of clinical psychology, medicine, anthropology, cultural studies, the educational sciences, and beyond.

Marianne Leuzinger-Bohleber, MD, Dr. Phil., is a former professor of psychoanalysis at the University of Kassel and director of the Sigmund-Freud-Institut, Frankfurt a.M. She is currently senior research fellow at the University Medicine Mainz, training analyst of the German Psychoanalytical Association (DPV/IPA), was vice chair of the Research Board of the IPA (2010–2021), and current member and former chair of the IPA Subcommittee for Migration and Refugees. She received the Mary Sigourney Award 2016, the Haskell Norman Prize for Excellence in Psychoanalysis 2017, the Robert S. Wallerstein Fellowship (2022–2027), and the IPA's Outstanding Scientific Achievement Award 2023.

Routledge Introductions to Contemporary Psychoanalysis

Aner Govrin, Ph.D.
Series Editor

Yael Peri Herzovich, Ph.D.
Executive Editor

"Routledge Introductions to Contemporary Psychoanalysis" is one of the prominent psychoanalytic publishing ventures of our day.

The series' aim is to become an encyclopedic enterprise of psychoanalysis, with each entry given its own book.

This comprehensive series is designed to illuminate the intricate landscape of psychoanalytic theory and practice. In this collection of concise yet illuminating volumes, we delve into the influential figures, groundbreaking concepts, and transformative theories that shape the contemporary psychoanalytic landscape.

At the heart of each volume lies a commitment to clarity, accessibility, and depth. Our expert authors, renowned scholars and practitioners in their respective fields guide readers through the complexities of psychoanalytic thought with precision and enthusiasm. Whether you are a seasoned psychoanalyst, a student eager to explore the field, or a curious reader seeking insight into the human psyche, our series offers a wealth of knowledge and insight.

Each volume serves as a gateway into a specific aspect of psychoanalytic theory and practice. From the pioneering works of Sigmund Freud to the innovative contributions of modern theorists such as Antonino Ferro and Michal Eigen, our series covers a diverse range of topics, including seminal figures, key concepts, and emerging trends. Whether you are interested in classical psychoanalysis, object relations theory, or the intersection of neuroscience and psychoanalysis, you will find a wealth of resources within our collection.

One of the hallmarks of our series is its interdisciplinary approach. While rooted in psychoanalytic theory, our volumes draw upon insights from psychology, philosophy, sociology, and other disciplines to offer a holistic understanding of the human mind and its complexities.

Each volume in the series is crafted with the reader in mind, balancing scholarly rigor with engaging prose. Whether you are embarking on your journey into psychoanalysis or seeking to deepen your understanding of specific topics, our series provides a clear and comprehensive roadmap.

Moreover, our series is committed to fostering dialogue and debate within the psychoanalytic community. Each volume invites readers to critically engage with the material, encouraging reflection, discussion, and further exploration.

We invite you to join us on this journey of discovery as we explore the ever-evolving landscape of psychoanalysis.

Aner Govrin - Editor

Marion Milner: A Contemporary Introduction
Alberto Stefana and Alessio Gamba

James F. Masterson: A Contemporary Introduction
Loray Daws

Antonino Ferro: A Contemporary Introduction
Robert Snell

Transgenerational Trauma: A Contemporary Introduction
Jill Salberg and Sue Grand

Schizophrenia: A Contemporary Introduction
Gillian Steggles

Erotic Transferences: A Contemporary Introduction
Andrea Celenza

Erich Fromm: A Contemporary Introduction
Sandra Buechler

The Death Drive: A Contemporary Introduction
Rossella Valdrè

Depression: A Contemporary Introduction
Marianne Leuzinger-Bohleber

Depression

A Contemporary Introduction

Marianne Leuzinger-Bohleber

Routledge
Taylor & Francis Group

LONDON AND NEW YORK

Designed cover image: Michal Heiman, Asylum 1855-2020,
The Sleeper (video, psychoanalytic sofa and Plate 34),
exhibition view, Herzliya Museum of Contemporary Art,
2017

First published 2025
by Routledge
4 Park Square, Milton Park, Abingdon, Oxon OX14 4RN

and by Routledge
605 Third Avenue, New York, NY 10158

*Routledge is an imprint of the Taylor & Francis Group, an
informa business*

British Library Cataloguing-in-Publication Data
A catalogue record for this book is available from the
British Library

ISBN: 9781032595979 (hbk)
ISBN: 9781032595962 (pbk)
ISBN: 9781003455349 (ebk)

DOI: 10.4324/9781003455349

Typeset in Times New Roman
by KnowledgeWorks Global Ltd.

Contents

Depression

A Contemporary Introduction

This is a long-awaited book integrating our contemporary understanding of depression, our most widespread psychological disorder—it has been called "the common cold" of mental illness. Depression seems strongly on the rise—we are much more likely to become depressed than were our grandparents—and the prescription rate of antidepressant drugs is rising dramatically. In this cultural context, there is an urgent need for better understanding and treatment of depression. As an excellent and most highly merited researcher and experienced clinician professor, Marianne Leuzinger-Bohleber in this book draws on 40 years of psychoanalytic research on depression, including follow-up as well as comparative studies. In a most impressive way, the book combines in-depth case studies, that is, clinical research, with extra-clinical empirical research in an interdisciplinary exchange with, for example, sociocultural contributions, neuroscience, developmental studies, and memory research. Specifically, the relationship between chronic severe depression and early trauma is explored. The book demonstrates the value of a psychoanalytic approach that goes beyond symptoms, addressing the suffering of human beings, their life histories, and existential situations—with deep empathy for the human condition. It is an excellent and unique contribution.

Oslo, January 2024
Siri Erika Gullestad,
Professor emeritus, Dr. Philos., University of Oslo, Norway
Chair, IPA Research Committee

Preface

Salman Rushdie's received the Peace Prize of the German Book Trade on October 24, 2023. In his impressive speech, he formulated the following in this context *"We should continue to do with renewed vigor what we have always had to do: counter bad speech with better speech, counter false narratives with better ones, respond to hate with love and never give up hope that the truth can prevail even in a time of lies."* (FAZ Feuilleton, 24.10.2023, translation MLB). His statement encouraged me in these weeks after the terrible attack by Hamas on Israel on October 7 and its appalling massacre, which left me horrified, paralyzed, and filled with great helplessness and powerlessness, to turn back to writing this book despite all the horror and the numbness in the face of these unimaginable atrocities and all the cruelties which followed.

Rushdie's statements lead directly to the topic I would like to discuss here. Heavily scarred by an attempted murder fueled by religious hatred, which he barely survived, his subtle humor and unpretentious, authentic plea to respond to hatred with love and not to give up hope that truth can prevail even in a time of lies touched me and many others deeply and acted as a unifying gesture of comfort and confidence.

Many individuals who have experienced similar extreme trauma as Salman Rushdie can no longer find their way back to such a comforting connection with others: they lose their basic trust in a loving and caring support from a helpful object as well as their own self, which collapses under the unimaginable atrocities that human beings can do to other human beings. Their psyche never stands up again: these individuals can hardly find their way back to the present. They lose their sense of time, continuity, and meaning in life. They react with depressive resignation and even withdraw into chronic depression.

As will be discussed, three large psychoanalytic depression studies (cf. Section 1.5) have shown that most individuals who suffer from severe depression have experienced severe early trauma: chronic depression seems to be an unconscious attempt by many to protect themselves from a new catastrophe, a new traumatization, by withdrawing psychically. It is better to do without light, hope, and vitality than to be disappointed again, to lose feelings of happiness and a fragile connection with others once more. *"I feel like a hermit crab, alone and mostly at home in a bleak existence in a gloomy cave, but at least safe from attack, injury and catastrophe ... "* (as Mrs B put it in a psychoanalytical session). The analytical work enabled her to find her own metaphors to describe her mental state, into which she had retreated as an eight-year-old after finding her father dead following a heart attack. (cf. Leuzinger-Bohleber et al., 2019).

As is well known, one of the characteristics of psychoanalysis is that traumatized individuals dare to approach the previously unimaginable horror of the trauma in the professional, holding and containing relationship with the analyst and to decode the associated, previously unconscious "embodied memories." Although the consequences of traumatization can never be erased, the associated symptoms are given meaning and are no longer perceived as mental foreign bodies: one's own trauma history becomes part of the idiosyncratic biography, of self and identity, the "false narrative" is replaced by a better one (cf. Leuzinger-Bohleber et al., 2019).

Since in psychoanalysis, in contrast to many other therapeutic approaches, such meaning-creating self and identity-finding processes are at the center of therapeutic work, the insights gained in the process can often be best captured and communicated in narratives. We have therefore included shorter or more detailed narratives in all publications of the major depression studies. In both the Follow-Up Study of the German Psychoanalytic Association (DPV) and the comparative outcome study of psychoanalytic and cognitive-behavioral long-term-psychotherapies, the LAC Depression Study, we also published detailed case histories in separate volumes (Leuzinger-Bohleber, Grabhorn & Bahrke, 2020). I regard them as core pieces of so-called clinical research in psychoanalysis and will therefore also draw on a relatively detailed case presentation in this introductory volume on depression (4).

Our research group has always combined clinical research in psychoanalysis with extra-clinical empirical research, also in order to measure the outcomes of psychoanalysis and long-term psychoanalytic treatment considering the criteria of evidence-based medicine. We have reported on these studies in numerous publications. Finally, we have combined the results of both clinical and extra-clinical psychoanalytic research on depression with so-called conceptual research in psychoanalysis. Three Joseph Sandler Research Conferences of the International Psychoanalytic Association (IPA) were dedicated to the topic of depression combining all these different research approaches to depression.

2005: *Depression* in London (local chair: Peter Fonagy).
2019: *Psychoanalytic Understanding and Treatment of Depression, Researchers and Clinicians in Dialogue* in Buenos Aires (local chair: Susana de Fischbein Vinocur).
2020: *On the Dark Side of Depression. Understanding the Subjective Experience of Patients with Chronic Depression: Psychoanalytic, Neurobiological and Sociocultural Perspectives* in Lausanne (local chair: Gilles Ambresin).

In this contemporary introduction on depression, I can therefore draw on, quote from, summarize, or refer to numerous publications on almost 40 years of psychoanalytic research on depression (see acknowledgments).

With this volume, I hope to provide an insight into the current state of psychoanalytic views on the genesis and psychodynamics of depression and its therapeutic treatment, but also to open our eyes to the state of discussions about this modern widespread disease in other disciplines. Treatment-related issues cannot be discussed comprehensively in this context. I would like to refer to the treatment manual for the MODE Study, the ongoing subsequent study of the LAC Study, by Leuzinger-Bohleber, Fischmann, and Beutel (2022), which we hope will soon be published in both English and French.

Overview

Thus, the focus of this volume is on a *psychoanalytic* perspective on depression, which differs from cognitive-behavioral conceptualizations and treatment of depressive disorders, for example, in conceptualizing the close connection between early traumatization and later, severe depression (cf., e.g., Krakau et al., 2023). Of course, this is not the only perspective. As explained in the introductory Chapter 1, depression is now regarded as a complex, polymorphic, and heterogeneous disorder that requires genetic, neurobiological, socio-psychological, cultural as well as individual-biographical explanations. Each of these explanations sheds light on different information structures of one of the most common and multifaceted mental illnesses affecting people today, as will be briefly discussed in Chapter 2. The current psychoanalytic understanding of depression emphasizes the close connection between trauma and depression, as will first be elaborated with reference to the psychotherapy studies already mentioned (Section 3.1). In our opinion, clinical and conceptual research in psychoanalysis has long tended to underestimate this connection and its consequences for the transgenerational transmission of severe depression and trauma (Section 3.2/3.3). As postulated in this volume on the basis of our own research findings, feelings of guilt or shame are less central to the psychic experience of chronic depressive illnesses today than the experience of extreme powerlessness, helplessness, and hopelessness. Due to unconscious early traumatization, chronic depressives react seismographically and particularly intensively to current, individual, and social situations in which the self has hardly any active options and solutions to offer and is flooded with diffuse fear, powerlessness, and helplessness. This is illustrated clinically shortly summarizing a psychoanalysis with a chronically depressed, early traumatized patient (Chapter 4).

The case study shows that depression can occur at any age, although around 50% of patients become intensely ill before the age of 31. In view of the risk of depression becoming chronic, intensive psychoanalytic treatment in childhood, adolescence, and early adulthood is therefore particularly relevant (Section 5.1/5.2). Further brief case studies illustrate that psychoanalysis in middle age can mitigate or, in the best case, even interrupt the transgenerational transmission of depression and trauma (Section 5.3) and that a depressive coloration of the view of one's own life in later adulthood can be relativized. From this perspective, the boundary between therapies and prevention is fluid, as suggested by both interdisciplinary research findings (Chapter 6) and a brief summary of experiences with early prevention projects (Chapter 7).

Frankfurt, October 2023
Marianne Leuzinger-Bohleber

References

Krakau, L., Ernst, M., Hautzinger, M., Beutel, M., & Leuzinger-Bohleber, M. (2023). *Long-term psychotherapy of chronic depression and early trauma: Differential benefits of psychoanalytic compared to cognitive behavioral treatments.* accepted for publication by the British Journal of Psychiatry Submitted.

Leuzinger-Bohleber, M., Ambresin, G., Fischmann, T., & Solms, M. (Eds.) (2022). *On the Dark Side. Understanding the Subjective Experience of Patients with Chronic Depression: Psychoanalytic, Neurobiological and Sociocultural Perspectives.* London: Routledge.

Leuzinger-Bohleber, M., Fischmann, T., & Beutel, M. E. (2022). *Chronische Depression. Psychoanalytische Langzeittherapie.* Reihe: Praxis der psychodynamischen Psychotherapie – analytische und tiefenpsychologisch fundierte Psychotherapie, Bd. 12. Göttingen: Hogrefe Verlag.

Leuzinger-Bohleber, M., Grabhorn, A., & Bahrke, U. (Eds.) (2020). *What Can Only Be Told and Not Measured.* Gießen: Psychosozial-Verlag.

Leuzinger-Bohleber, M., Kaufhold, J., Kallenbach, L., Negele, A., Ernst, M., Keller, W., & Beutel, M. (2019). How to measure sustained psychic transformations in long-term treatments of chronically depressed patients: Symptomatic and structural changes in the LAC Depression Study of the outcome of cognitive-behavioural and psychoanalytic long-term treatments. *The International Journal of Psychoanalysis, 100*(1), 99–127.

Acknowledgments

I was delighted to be asked to contribute a volume on depression to the Introduction to Contemporary Psychoanalysis series. It gives me the opportunity to summarize our psychoanalytic insights into this widespread illness from several decades of clinical, conceptual, and empirical research on depression. Today's research in all scientific disciplines has become a demanding, international, and interdisciplinary undertaking that can hardly be accomplished by a single person, but usually only by many in scientific and personal networks. I would therefore like to thank many people who have participated in these years of research work and whom I unfortunately cannot mention here all by name.

My thanks go above all to the several hundred chronically depressed patients who placed their trust in me and our research teams in my psychoanalytic practice and the large depression studies in order to explore together the unconscious sources of their severe mental suffering.

All of these projects were, or are, an intergenerational endeavor in which experienced clinicians and researchers worked closely with the next generation of clinical and scientific trainees and representatives of practice and other disciplines. I would therefore like to thank many of those who have contributed to and supported the research projects summarized in this volume. My thanks goes

- To the more than 200 study therapists of the three depression studies.
- To the directors of the MODE centers (Erwin Sturm, Lisa Kallenbach-Kaminski, Andju Labuhn, Elisabeth Imhorst, Christine Huth, Serge Croes, Sylvia Janko-Milch, Cheryl Goodrich, Klaus Poppensieker, Gilles Ambresin, and others).

- To the intergenerational and international research networks with generations of student assistants, Master's students, doctoral students, and postdoctoral researchers.
- To the administrative and scientific co-directors, especially my co-director at the Sigmund-Freud-Institut (SFI) Rolf Haubl, and the co-project leaders Ulrich Stuhr, Manfred Beutel, Martin Hautzinger, Wolfram Keller, Georg Fiedler and now Bradley Peterson, Tamara Fischmann, Gilles Ambresin, Cheryl Goodrich, Charles Fischer, Karl Poppensieker and for the STEP-BY-STEP Project: Sabine Andresen, Marcus Hasselhorn.
- To members of the scientific team: Ulrich Bahrke, Lisa Kallenbach-Kaminski, Alexa Negele, Simon Arnold, Anne Schorr, Nicoletta Zuccharini, Patrick Stier, Paula Rehm, Fatima Nöske, Stephan Hau, Heinrich Deserno, Judith Lebiger-Vogel, Constanze Rickmeyer, Korinna Fritzemeyer, Lorena Asseburg, Verena Neubert, Inka Werner, Birgit Gaertner, Katrin Luise Laezer, Nora Hettich, Mariam Tahiri, and others, as well as the many of our students and part-time employees.
- To the colleagues and study therapists of the Anna Freud Institute (AFI) (especially Angelika Wolff, Claudia Burkhardt-Mussmann, and Heidi Staufenberg) and supporters of the city of Frankfurt (especially the former mayor Jutta Ebeling).
- To the international dialogue and cooperation partners, including Ulrich Moser, Rolf Pfeifer, Dieter Bürgin, Hugo Bleichmar, Robert Wallerstein, Peter Fonagy, Mary Hepworth, David Taylor, Mark Solms, Rolf Sandell, Horst Kächele, Ulrich Stuhr, Siri Gullestad, Sverre Varvin, Robert Emde, Henri Parens, Heinz Böker, Johannes Lethonen, Jorge Ahumada, Michael Hampe, Jorge Canestri, Daniel Widlöcher, Steven Roose, Charles Fischer, Harriet Wolfe, Gilbert Kliman, Juan Pablo Jimenez, Judy Kantowitz, Ricardo Bernardi, Dominique Scarfone, Heribert Blass, Jean Nicolas Despland, and others.
- To the financial supporters: e.g., EU, DFG, DGPT, DPV, IPA, APsA, Alfred Berman Foundation, R. S. Wallerstein Fellowship, Matthias von der Tann, Hertie Foundation, Polytechnische Gesellschaft, Zinnkann Foundation, Crespo Foundation, and Heidehof Foundation.
- To the administrative team of the University of Kassel and the Sigmund-Freud-Institut, Ute Ochtendung, Renate Stebahne, Panja Schweder, Herbert Bareuther, and many others.

Finally, special thanks go to Ute Ochtendung for helping to shape this manuscript and to my dear friend and colleague, Siri Gullestad, Chair of the Research Committee of the International Psychoanalytical Association (IPA).

All my reflections and insights from clinical practice and research, which I present for discussion in this volume, were enriched by the daily exchange with Werner Bohleber. A precious gift!

Frankfurt, October 2023
Marianne Leuzinger-Bohleber

Depression as a common, polymorphic, heterogeneous disease with a tendency to chronicity

Introductory remarks

I was referred to a certain Dr. Wayne Myers in New York City, an avuncular, soft-spoken man with a gentle smile. For the next twenty-five years, Doc Myers and I would battle my demons in countless sessions and longdistance conversations until his death in 2008. Whenever I was in town, we would sit across from each other, I would look patiently into his understanding eyes, and painstakingly we would achieve a remarkable series of successes, but also experience a few harsh setbacks. We clearly slowed down the treadmill I was on, even if it never came to a complete standstill. Doc Myers' practice was my home port in the new odyssey I was embarking on. His knowledge and compassion gave me the inner strength and freedom I needed to truly love and be loved …

(Bruce Springsteen,[1] 2016, Translation from the German book to English MLB, p. 418)

1.1 What is a psychoanalytical understanding of depression?

Depression[2] is an affective disorder characterized by a deeply painful mood, a loss of interest in the outside world, a loss of the ability to love, the inhibition of every achievement and the lowering of self-esteem, which manifests itself in self-reproach and self-abuse (Freud, 1916/17f., p. 429). There is a wide range of variation in the symptoms and course of the different states of depression. The classification of depressive disorders has always been controversial and has not been clearly resolved to this day. Instead of assuming a homogeneous clinical picture, it is in any case appropriate to speak of a heterogeneous group of depression. In the respective pathogenesis, somatic-biological, psychogenic

DOI: 10.4324/9781003455349-1

and social factors are intertwined to varying degrees. From a psychoanalytical point of view, every depressive shows a more or less pronounced and typical psychodynamic. The group of depressives is one of the best-studied clinical pictures; today, depressives represent the largest patient group in psychoanalytic therapy.

(Will et al., 2008, p. 130/131, Translation MLB)

Twenty to thirty-three percent of people with a depressive disorder develop a chronic course (Hölzel et al., 2011; Malhi & Mann, 2018). Patients suffering from chronic depression are particularly likely to experience severe depression, depressive episodes, and psychiatric and physical comorbidities. Compared to other depressed patients, they take psychotropic drugs for longer and have a lower remission rate. Chronic depression is also associated with enormous suffering for those affected and their families, as well as high direct and indirect healthcare costs (see, among others, Milton, 2001; Moussavi et al., 2007; Trivedi, Nieuwsma & Williams, 2011; De Maat et al., 2013; Leuzinger-Bohleber, Arnold & Kächele, 2015/2019; Gibbons et al., 2016; Schramm et al., 2017; Cuijpers, Huibers & Furukawa, 2017; Cuijpers et al., 2021; Leuzinger-Bohleber, Fischmann & Beutel, 2022).

The following case example may briefly illustrate the characteristics of a depressive illness, the risk of chronification, the close link between trauma and depression, and the transgenerational dimension.

"... a big, dark wave comes and pulls me out ..."

A 55-year-old retired employee, Mrs A, was referred to the LAC (Psychoanalytische und kognitiv-verhaltenstherapeutische **La**ngzeittherapien bei **c**hronischer depression [Psychoanalytic and cognitive-behavioral Longtermtherapies with chronic depression]) study (see Section 1.5) after a several-month inpatient stay in a psychiatric hospital. "I can no longer work ... After the death of my mother 2 years ago, I completely collapsed, just lying in bed, unable to sleep or eat ... After a suicide attempt, my husband admitted me to the hospital ... There I gradually felt a little better … I would have preferred to stay there … I was afraid of completely collapsing again or of swallowing too many pills again in panic." Already in the first interview she reported her initial dream in which her suicidality or death wish comes out: "I am standing by the sea—a big, dark wave comes and pulls me out … I do not resist, but find it beautiful to surrender to it …"

Mrs A suffered from severe depression since childhood. Her mother was a German war child of World War II with a "difficult personality." She suffered from Alzheimer's disease for 10 years until she finally died. During this time, she demanded that the patient always be available to her and take care of her. She was often violent and extremely aggressive toward the patient.

Mrs A is the second of five children in a poor migrant family from Southern Europe. She recalled several traumatic separation experiences as a young child, including a life-threatening illness during summer vacation when she was "left in a convent" at age 4.

Later, when the patient was 14 years old, her father's business had to declare bankruptcy. The family "fled" to Germany, which meant that the patient had to drop out of school and all social relations and start an apprenticeship.

During the treatment, based on dreams, memory fragments, and finally confirmations by her siblings, the traumatic experience became tangible that Mrs A had been regularly sexually abused by her father during his "nap" at the age of 5–12. However, the patient's hatred (unconscious and gradually becoming conscious) was mainly directed against her mother "for sending me to nap with the father …" (Mrs A).

At the age of 16, Mrs A experienced another sexual abuse at the hands of her boss. "I escaped into marriage and had two children … motherhood kept me going ever since …" (Mrs A).

In the psychoanalytic treatment, it became clear that Mrs A had developed too few stable inner boundaries between the self and object representations, as well as between the generations: the generations were telescoped into each other

(Faimberg, 1987). In addition, the sexual or psychological abuse by both parents had destroyed her basic trust in helping others and the self's ability to defend itself, which could finally be understood in the therapeutic relationship and successively worked on therapeutically. It was impressive how this finally enabled Mrs A to mourn her mother's death, thus diminishing the unconscious suicidal impulse to follow her to her death. Parallel to this, her relationship with her adult children gradually improved, from whom she learned to better separate herself inwardly and outwardly, and thus experienced them less as parasitic and exploitative.

1.2   Definition according to IDC-10 and DSM-V

In the International Classification System (ICD)-10, depressive disorders are defined under the category of affective disorders. The main symptoms are changes in mood (affectivity) and activity level. Major depressive episodes and mania form the poles of the entire spectrum from severe low mood, loss of interest, and joylessness to elevated or irritable mood in mania (S3 National Health Care Guidelines [NVL] Unipolar Depression) (https://www.leitlinien.de/nvl/html/depression/kapitel-2).

1.2.1   Depressive episodes

The ICD-10 distinguishes between mild (F32.0), moderate (F32.1), and severe (F32.2) depressive episodes; it is also coded whether the episodes are single (F32.x) or recurrent (F33.x). The severity of the depressive disorder is based on the number of main and additional symptoms met (mild depressive episode text box). A mild depressive episode requires at least two of the three main symptoms or four or five of the symptoms from B and C together. A moderate depressive episode according to ICD-10 (F32.1) requires a total of six to seven symptoms, and a major depressive episode (F32.2) requires all three main symptoms and at least eight symptoms in total. In a major depressive episode, a further distinction can be made as to whether psychotic symptoms (ego-syntonic delusions of sin, impoverishment, or impending catastrophe; accusatory hallucinations, depressive stupor) are present.

Criteria for a mild depressive episode according to ICD-10 (World Health Organization (WHO), 2006, p. 106f., authors transl. from German to English):

A. The general criteria for a depressive episode are met (duration of at least two weeks, criteria for manic or hypomanic episode not met, episode not due to abuse of psychic substances or organic mental disorder).
B. At least two of the following three symptoms are present:

   1. Depressed mood; to a degree that is clearly unusual for those affected, most of the day, almost every day, essentially unaffected by circumstances.
   2. Loss of interest or pleasure in activities that were normally enjoyable.
   3. Decreased drive or increased fatigability.

C. One or more additional of the following symptoms up to a total of B and C of at least four or five symptoms:

   1. Loss of self-confidence or self-esteem.
   2. Unfounded self-blame or pronounced inappropriate guilt.
   3. Recurrent thoughts of death or suicide or suicidal behavior.
   4. Complaints of or evidence of decreased ability to think or concentrate, indecision, or indecisiveness.
   5. Psychomotor agitation or inhibition (subjective or objective).
   6. Sleep disorders of any kind.
   7. Loss of appetite or increased appetite with corresponding change in weight.

In addition, the fifth digit can be used to code whether a somatic syndrome is present for all depressive episodes. For this, at least four symptoms from the corresponding list must be present (see text box).

Somatic syndrome (WHO, 2006, p. 106):

1. Marked loss of interest or enjoyment in normally pleasurable activities.
2. Lack of ability to respond emotionally to events or activities that would normally be responded to.
3. Waking up early, two hours or more, before the usual time.
4. Morning low.
5. Objective findings of marked psychomotor inhibition or agitation.
6. Significant loss of appetite.
7. Weight loss (5% or more of body weight in the past month).
8. Significant loss of libido.

Recurrent depressive episodes may be coded as recurrent depressive disorder if the full depressive episode is not present in the interim.

The DSM-5 (Diagnostic and Statistical Manual of Mental Disorders, 5th ed.; American Psychiatric Association [APA], 2013) has largely adopted the DSM-IV criteria for depressive disorders, as illustrated by major depression (authors' transl; text box).

Major depression according to DSM-5 (p. 160f.):

A. Five or more of the symptoms present for a period of 2 weeks; deviation from previous functional status; at least one symptom affects the first or second symptom.

1. Depressed mood most of the day, almost every day (feels sad, empty, and hopeless).
2. Significantly decreased interest or pleasure in all or nearly all activities (most/most every day).

3. Significant weight loss or weight gain (more than 5% in one month), or altered appetite almost every day.
4. Insomnia or hypersomnia.
5. Psychomotor agitation or slowing (observable by others).
6. Exhaustion or loss of energy almost every day.
7. Feelings of worthlessness or excessive or inappropriate guilt almost every day.
8. Decreased ability to think or concentrate, or lack of resolution, almost every day.
9. Recurrent thoughts of dying, suicidal ideation without specific plan, suicide attempt, or specific plan.

B. Significant clinical distress or impairment in social, occupational, or other important areas of functioning.
C. Not explainable by substance use or other medical conditions.
D. Not better explained by illness from the schizophrenic forms.
E. No manic or hypomanic episode.

Symptoms can be divided into emotional symptoms (1, 2, 7, 9), neurovegetative symptoms (3, 4, 6), and neurocognitive symptoms (5, 8).

1.2.2 Persistent depressive disorder (dysthymia)

It is a long-lasting (chronic) and fluctuating depressive mood disorder in which individual depressive episodes do not usually meet the criteria for a mild or moderate depressive episode. Because it sometimes persists for the greater part of adult life, it entails considerable subjective suffering and impairment. A depressive episode may override the persistent affective disorder (so-called "double depression").

A dysthymia (ICD-10: F34.1) is defined as follows (WHO, 2006, p. 112f.):

A constant or consistently recurring depression over a period of at least two years.

B none or very few of the individual depressive episodes during such a two-year period are severe enough or last long
enough to meet the criteria for recurrent mild depressive
disorder (ICD-10: F33.0).
C at least some periods of depression, at least three of the following symptoms should be present:

1. Decreased drive or activity.
2. Pronounced sleep disorders.
3. Loss of self-confidence or feeling of inadequacy.
4. Concentration difficulties.
5. Social withdrawal.
6. Loss of interest or pleasure in sexuality and other pleasurable activities.
7. Decreased talkativeness.
8. Pessimism about the future or brooding about the past.
9. Recognizable inability to cope with the routine demands of daily life.
10. Tendency to cry.
11. Feeling of hopelessness and despair.

For the distinctions between ICD-10 and DSM-V, see NVL Unipolar Depression (Section 2.2.2.1).

1.3 Epidemiology

In recent decades, depression has increased to such an extent that, according to WHO estimates, it has become the third most common widespread
disease, with an upward trend. Its individual and social significance is
still underestimated. The risk of developing depression at least once in a
lifetime is 16–20% internationally. The 12-month prevalence of unipolar
depression is about 7.7% (women 10.6% and men 4.8%), of depressive
episodes (major depression) about 6%, in men about 3.4%, in women
8.4%. In 2023, worldwide 280 million people are suffering from depression. Women are twice as likely as men to suffer from depression, but the
risk of depression has also increased in men in recent years. Compared
to the 1998 Health Survey, prevalence rates have remained stable. However, it has been shown that younger women have suffered from severe

depression more frequently in recent years and that men are also increasingly suffering from severe depression (Nationale Leitlinie Unipolare Depression (NVL), 2022, p. 18ff.). Depression occurs at any age: 50% before age 31. Depression in children and adolescents has been on the rise for several years: the increase was particularly strong in the months of the pandemic. However, it is also very common among older people and the elderly (high suicide rates among very old men) (NVL, 2022, p. 18ff.). In older age, depression is the most common mental illness, often combined with physical illness and functional impairment. Suicide rates also increase with age and are highest among the very old.

Data from health insurance in Germany shows that in 2009, 12.5% of patients who received outpatient and inpatient treatment were diagnosed with depression; in 2017, the figure was 15.7%. This may indicate that people with depression are increasingly recognizing their illness and undergoing treatment. It is possible that the broad-based media campaign has contributed to a certain removal of taboos surrounding depressive illnesses.

1.4 Socio-economic data

Some socio-economic factors are now well studied: higher levels of education and job security correlate with lower rates of depression. People from lower social classes are particularly likely to suffer from depression. In addition, people from an urban population who are not in a stable relationship, divorced, or widowed are at an increased risk of depression. Recent studies have also shown that women are around twice as likely to suffer from depression as men. Low social support, isolation and marginalization, stressful life events, and chronic illness are risk factors (Tibubos et al., 2020). Epidemiological studies show that 15–30% of people with depression become chronic. After the third depressive episode, the relapse rate is 90%.

1.5 Treatability and psychotherapy— Outcome studies

For a long time, depression was regarded as an illness with a relatively good prognosis for treatment, an assessment that must now be differentiated. For example, low-threshold services, crisis interventions, and short-term behavioral and psychoanalytic therapies have a good effect on many depressive patients if it is a first illness triggered by a crisis-related life event. However, relapse rates are enormously high in a relatively large group of patients to both any form of brief psycho- therapy (50%) and drug treatments (see Blatt, 2004; Blatt & Zuroff, 2005; Hölzel et al., 2011; Steinert et al., 2014, 2017; Cuijpers et al., 2017, 2021; Cuijpers, Reijnders & Huibers, 2019; Malhi & Mann, 2018; NVL, 2022, p. 24).

Since 20–30% of all depressed patients do not respond positively to medication at all (see, e.g., Trivedi et al., 2011; Corveleyn et al., 2013; Huhn et al., 2014), there have recently been heated debates about the use of antidepressants. Even the authors of the recently completed re- vision of the "Nationale Versorgungsleitlinie: Unipolare Depression für Erwachsene (NVL)" (National Health Care Guideline Unipolar Depression for Adults) in Germany have taken seriously the method- critical reassessments of large pharmaceutical studies by some scientists who fundamentally question the clinical relevance of antidepressants (e.g., Munkholm, Paludan-Müller & Boesen, 2019; Hengartner, 2019). Indeed, recent research has shown that it is questionable whether—as previously assumed—monoamine deficiency is the cause of depres- sive illness (Gold, Machado-Vieira & Pavlatou, 2015).

Almost all antidepressants available in Germany are based on the the- ory of such a deficiency and increase the concentration of monoamines (serotonin, noradrenaline, possibly also dopamine) in the synaptic cleft in different ways. It can therefore be assumed that other, as yet unknown mechanisms are (partly) responsible for the effectiveness of antidepres- sants. For example, some of the new developments in antidepressants target the glutamate system associated with the stress axis (e.g., keta- mine/esketamine) (cf. Gold, Machado-Vieira & Pavlatou, 2015).

Despite this currently only weakly empirically supported effect of antidepressants, the guideline adheres to a combination treatment of medication and psychotherapy in severe depression (p. 99)[3] (see also Leichsenring, 2008; Leichsenring & Rabung, 2011; Rabung & Leichsenring, 2016; Bach, Kerber & Aluja, 2020; Cuijpers et al., 2019, 2021; Leichsenring et al., 2021a, 2021b).

Apparently, little consideration was given to the fact that the psy- choanalytic research landscape has changed a great deal in the last 30 years and that many large international psychotherapy studies have now demonstrated that about three-quarters of chronically depressed patients not only achieve lasting relief of their depressive symptoms through long-term psychoanalytic treatment, but also a sustained improvement in their social relationships, their ability to work, and their quality of life. In addition, relapses can be prevented and often without a combination with medication. Publically it does not seem to be known that in the last decades, many international psychoanalytic research groups have taken on the enormous challenge of not only empirically investigating the effectiveness of brief therapies, but have also taken on the great time, personnel, and financial burden of investigating long-term psychoanalytic therapies and psychoanalyses. All of these research groups had also conducted intensive epistemological and methodological debates during these years, among other things to motivate clinicians to study their ongoing psychoanalyses empirically.

Thirty years ago, at the time of the Follow-Up Study of the German Psychoanalytic Association (DPV), the majority of analysts were still very skeptical about empirical outcome studies for theoretical and methodological reasons. They argued that the specific research object of psychoanalysis, namely unconscious processes and fantasies, could not in principle be measured empirically. In doing so, they relied on important publications by Alfred Lorenzer, Jürgen Habermas, Paul Feyerabend, and George Devereux, to name just a few of the best-known (cf. Leuzinger-Bohleber, Solms & Arnold, 2020; Leuzinger-Bohleber, 2021).

We took these arguments very seriously when conceptualizing the DPV Follow-Up -Study and, together with the statistics professor Bernhard Rüger, developed a sophisticated design for a *retrospective* study, since at that time hardly any of our psychoanalytic colleagues would have been willing to empirically investigate ongoing psychoanalysis in a prospective design. An elaborate baseline survey allowed us to statistically prove the representativeness of the sample of 402 former psychoanalysis patients. We examined these patients using a combination of genuine psychoanalytic as well as internationally accepted psychotherapy research instruments. Since more than 70 DPV analysts were involved in the study, reported on the progress of the study at every general assembly of the DPV members, and engaged in many epistemological and methodological debates, there was great curiosity and interest in this type of research, so that the epistemological debates became more differentiated and produced less polarizing positions than in the 1990s. Encouragingly, this combination of methods also enabled us to show that between 70% and 80% of all patients achieved a sustained improvement in their condition on average 6.5 years after completing their therapies (according to their own statements, those of their therapists, independent assessors, and socio-economic data) (see Leuzinger-Bohleber et al., 2003)

The increased openness of DPV members to empirical outcome research made it possible to begin the first controlled, prospective psychotherapy study comparing the outcomes of psychoanalytic and cognitive-behavioral long-term psychotherapies in chronically depressed patients with randomized and preferential assignment, the LAC study, in 2005. In it, we defined psychoanalysis, or long-term psychoanalytic therapies—in contrast to behavioral therapy—as follows:

> Psychoanalytic therapy studies the influence that unconscious wishes and fears exert on conscious experience and action in the here and now. Psychoanalytic therapy does not, as is often assumed, stop at coming to terms with unresolved childhood experiences, but uncovers their unconscious and conscious effects in connection with biographical experiences, also with regard to shaping the future. Through the possibility of repeating unconscious object-relational pattern in the relationship with the analyst, psychoanalytic psychotherapy attempts to track down the significance of recurring depressive processing of life experiences. The sustainability of psychoanalytic psychotherapy can be seen in a subsequent development of one's own self-esteem and in the relationship with others. The symptoms change as an outcome of the analytical process, as the previously inadequate causes of the illness are uncovered, processed and integrated. The therapy can take place at a frequency of one to a maximum of five 50-minute sessions per week.
>
> (Information handed out to the interested patients
> in the LAC Study, translation MLB)

Briefly about the results: 554 chronically depressed patients were screened in the four treatment centers, and 252 could be included in the study. Both psychotherapy methods proved to be successful in achieving a significant reduction in symptoms in these patients, many of whom had been ill for a long time. The patients' self-assessments as well as blind to treatment ratings showed significant and stable changes.[4]

Contrary to our hypotheses, however, we found no statistically significant difference in regard to symptom reduction between the two treatment arms as well as between randomized and preferential treatment after three years of treatment. In addition, CBT (Cognitive Behavioral Therapy) was not more efficient in terms of symptom reduction after one year: PAT also led to a statistically significant symptom reduction after one year, which was not statistically different from that of CBT. However, contrary to our hypothesis, they were not superior in regard to symptom reduction to CBT up to T8, that is, up to three years after the start of treatment, but were equally effective. The remission rates achieved were better than in other studies: 39% of patients showed full remission after just one year, and 61% of patients showed full remission after three years from the start of treatment. Chronically depressed patients therefore benefit from long-term psychotherapy.

The second main publication summarized the so-called structural changes that are considered central to sustainable psychological changes in psychoanalysis and long-term psychoanalytic treatments. After three years, statistically significantly more patients in PAT (60%) met the criteria for structural change on the Heidelberg Restructuring Scale compared to CBT (36%). In addition, after three years, there was a stronger correlation between structural changes and reduction of depressive symptoms in PAT than in CBT.

Further analyses of data five years after the beginning of treatment show that patients with early trauma have better outcomes in PAT than in CBT (Krakau et al., 2023).

As in the DPV Follow-Up-Study the close connection between chronic depression and trauma was shown: 84% of the patients had stated that they had experienced early trauma. According to the assessment of their treating analysts, the number of severely traumatized patients was even higher (Negele et al., 2015).

In relation to the above-mentioned discussions in the Nationale Versorgungsleitlinie NVL, the LAC study showed that medication was only taken continuously throughout psychotherapy in around a quarter of cases (25.4%) (cf. Schiele & Kallenbach-Kaminski, unpublished manuscript, p. 9). In other patients, medication was used, for example, as additional support in (suicidal) crises. However the search for the complex, mostly unconscious meaning structures of the depressive reactions was at the center of the psychoanalytic treatments (cf. Küchenhoff, 2010). As we have described in various detailed case reports, the insights gained in this process often led to a lasting transformation of the patient's inner world, which is described in psychoanalysis as a structural change. We were also able to demonstrate empirically that in PAT(Psychoanalytic Treatments)—in contrast to behavioral therapy—after three and now also after five years, there was statistically significant evidence of patients' insight into such lasting, structural changes, which were linked to the symptom change but, as we know from the detailed case studies, went far beyond it (cf. Leuzinger-Bohleber et al., 2019b; Beutel et al., 2022).

Some large prospective studies, including some randomized studies, have since come to similar conclusions, e.g. the Stockholm study (Blomberg, 2001), the Frankfurt-Hamburg study (Brockmann, Schlüter & Eckert, 2006), the Göttingen study (Leichsenring et al., 2005), the Munich psychotherapy study (Huber & Klug, 2016), the PAL practice study on long-term analytical therapy (Rudolf et al., 2012), the Helsinki study (Knekt et al., 2011), the Tavistock depression study (Fonagy et al., 2015), and, as just mentioned, the LAC depression study (Leuzinger-Bohleber et al., 2019a, 2019b, Leuzinger-Bohleber, Solms & Arnold, 2020; Leuzinger-Bohleber, Grabhorn & Bahrke, 2020)

As all of these studies were very complex and costly and therefore—compared to pharmacological studies—could only include a limited number of patients, the Mainz MELAS study attempts to combine the data from all of these studies in a so-called individual participant meta-analysis in order to have sufficient statistical power to investigate the psychological and psychosocial changes in depressive patients in an even more differentiated way in order to determine which patients with which type of depression are most likely to be helped sustainably with which procedure (cf. Beutel, Leuzinger-Bohleber & Krakau, 2021).

Finally, the relationship between chronic depression and trauma is further investigated in an ongoing study, the MODE Study: **M**ultilevel **O**utcome Study of Psychoanalysis of Chronically **De**pressed Patients with Early Trauma ("MODE") (Leuzinger-Bohleber et al., 2022; Ambresin et al., 2023).

The MODE study builds on the results of the LAC depression study. In the LAC study, the psychoanalysts were free to decide in which treatment setting they wanted to conduct the psychoanalyses with these difficult-to-treat patients. One group of analysts decided to start with one sitting session per week and, once a basic trust in the analyst had developed, to increase the frequency of sessions and use the couch. Other analysts assumed that most of these patients had already undergone several (brief) therapies, an assumption that was confirmed. In total, 45% of all LAC patients had undergone two or more previous therapies. Therefore these psychoanalysts decided to work immediately in a high-frequency, couch setting. We observed both good and problematic courses in both groups. The MODE study therefore addresses the question of whether there are certain patient groups that require high-frequency treatments in order to be therapeutically accessible at all.

MODE therefore investigates the outcomes of high-frequency and low-frequency psychoanalysis in early traumatized, chronically depressed patients. Patients are randomly assigned to one of the two treatment conditions. A treatment manual is available for the study therapists. Treatment progress will be tracked in terms of symptom reduction (using standard psychological measures), structural change (defined by psychoanalytic methods), and neurobiological change (assessed by fMRI [Funktionelle Kernspintomographie: Functional magnetic resonance imaging]).

From October 2017 to December 2019, various feasibility studies were conducted to explore the potential for the MODE study. They showed that MODE is feasible on a multicenter basis. The study is currently being conducted in Germany (Frankfurt a.M., Cologne, Leipzig, Giessen, and Mainz), Switzerland (Lausanne), and the USA (San Francisco (Los Angeles)) (see Ambresin et al., 2023). By the July 2024, 112 chronic depressed patients with early trauma were in psychoanalysis, and 67 of them had also been investigated by fMRI. In total, 35 persons without depression have been investigated in the so-called "control-group." The recruitment of the patients and controls was finished by the end of March 2024.

We therefore hope that, due to the changed research situation, all these studies will be taken into account in the next revision of the NVL in Germany as well as in other countries, although we know that despite all these joint efforts by international psychoanalytic research groups, the political battles for the recognition of psychoanalysis in the healthcare system and at universities will probably continue. These debates not only have a scientific dimension but are, of course, embedded in political, social, and cultural contexts (see Section 2).

Notes

1 In his autobiography Born to Run, Bruce Springsteen describes how he suffered from depression throughout his life. Psychoanalysis repeatedly helped him to regain his creativity, which, as is so often the case with

artists, goes hand in hand with depressive illnesses—just think of some of the best-known examples such as Vincent Van Gogh, Eduard Munch, but also musicians such as Ludwig van Beethoven, Franz Schubert, and Gustav Mahler.

2   Some of the following sections are an English translation of Chapter 2, in Leuzinger-Bohleber, Fischmann and Beutel (2022, p. 26ff.), enriched by new information. Section 1.2 was written under the leadership of Manfred Beutel. In ICD-11, which will be published soon, some changes will be made, but these cannot yet be taken into account here.

3   Leichsenring, Steinert and Hoyer (2016) have shown in a meta-analysis that psychotherapy and pharmacotherapy are equally effective in terms of short-term outcomes, but that psychotherapy is more effective in the long term.

4   After just one year, the BDI (Beck Depression Inventory) value of 32.1 points decreased by 12.1 points, and after three years by as much as 17.2 points. The effect sizes were very high: $d = 1.17$ after one year and $d = 1.83$ after three years. The complete remission rate was already 34% after one year and rose to 45% after three years. Analogous results were seen in the assessments of the independent raters who were blinded to the treatment methods: the QIDS-C (Quick Inventory of Depressive Symptomatology, Clinical Rating) values fell from 14.1 to 7.1 in the first year and further to 7.0 three years after the start of treatment. The effect sizes were also very high: they increased from $d = 1.56$ at one year to $d = 2.08$ at three years after the start of treatment.

References

Ambresin, G., Leuzinger-Bohleber, M., Fischmann, T., Axmacher, N., Hattingen, E., Bansal, R., & Peterson, B. S. (2023). The multi-level outcome study of psychoanalysis for chronically depressed patients with early trauma (MODE), rationale and design of an international multicenter randomized controlled trial. *MBC Psychiatry*, accepted for publication, October 2023.

American Psychiatric Association. (2013). *Diagnostic and Statistical Manual of Mental Disorders* (5th ed.). Arlington, VA: American Psychiatric Association.

Bach, B., Kerber, A., Aluja, A., Fossati, A., Gutierres, F., Rolland, J.P., Roskam, I., Spanemberg, L., Strus, W., Thimm, J.C., Zimmermann, J., Bastiaens, T., Keeley, J.W., Claes, L., Oliveira, A., Sellbom, M., Pires, R., Riegel, K.D., Somma, A., & Wright, A. (2020). International assessment of DSM-5 and ICD-11 personality disorder traits: Toward a common nosology in DSM-5.1. *Psychopathology*, *53*(3–4), 179–188. https://doi.org/10.1159/000507589

Beutel, M. E., Krakau, L., Kaufhold, J., Bahrke, U., Grabhorn, A., Hautzinger, M., Fiedler, G., Kallenbach-Kaminski, L., Ernst, M., Rüger, B., & Leuzinger-Bohleber, M. (2022). Recovery from chronic depression and structural change: 5-year outcomes after psychoanalytic and cognitive-behavioural long-term treatments (LAC depression study). *Clinical Psychology & Psychotherapy*, *30*(1), 188–201. https://doi.org/10.1002/cpp.2793

Beutel, M. E., Leuzinger-Bohleber, M., & Krakau, L. (2021). *Wirksamkeit niedrig- und hochfrequenter psychoanalytisch fundierter langzeitbehandlungen. Meta-Analysis of Longtterm Analytic Treatment Study (MeLAS).* Unveröffentlichter Vortrag, Universitätsmedizin Mainz.

Blatt, S. J. (2004). *Experiences of Depression: Theoretical, Clinical, and Research Perspectives.* New York: American Psychological Association.

Blatt, S. J., & Zuroff, D. C. (2005). Empirical evaluation of the assumptions in identifying evidence-based treatments in mental health. *Clinical Psychology Review, 25*(4), 459–486.

Blomberg, J. (2001). Long-term outcome of long-term psychoanalytically oriented therapies: First findings of the Stockholm outcome of psychotherapy and psychoanalysis study. *Psychotherapy Research, 11*(4), 361–382.

Brockmann, J., Schlüter, T., & Eckert, J. (2006). Langzeitwirkungen psychoanalytischer und verhaltenstherapeutischer Langzeitpsychotherapien: Eine vergleichende Studie aus der Praxis niedergelassener Psychotherapeuten [Long-term effects of long-term psychoanalytic and long-term behavior therapy. A comparative study from the general practices of psychotherapists]. *Psychotherapeut, 51*, 15–25. https://doi.org/10.1007/s00278-005-0454-x

Corveleyn, J., Luyten, P., Blatt, S. J., & Lens-Gielis, H. (2013). *The Theory and Treatment of Depression: Towards a Dynamic Interactionism Model.* Routledge.

Cuijpers, P., Huibers, M. J. H., & Furukawa, T. A. (2017). The need for research on treatments of chronic depression. *JAMA Psychiatry, 74*(3), 242–243. https://doi.org/10.1001/jamapsychiatry.2016.4070

Cuijpers, P., Reijnders, M., & Huibers, M. J. H. (2019). The role of common factors in psychotherapy outcomes. *Annual Review Clinical Psychology, 15*, 207–231.

Cuijpers, P., Pineda, B. S., Quero, S., Karyotaki, E., Struijs, S. Y., Figueroa, C. A., & Muñoz, R. F. (2021). Psychological interventions to prevent the onset of depressive disorders: A meta-analysis of randomized controlled trials. *Clinical Psychology Review, 83*, 101955.

De Maat, S., de Jonghe, F., de Kraker, R., Leichsenring, F., Abbass, A., Luyten, P., & Dekker, J. (2013). The current state of the empirical evidence for psychoanalysis: A meta-analytic approach. *Harvard Review of Psychiatry, 21*, 107–137.

Faimberg, H. (1987). The telescoping of generations. On the genealogy of certain identifications. *Yearbook of Psychoanalysis, 20*(S), 114–142.

Fonagy, P., Rost, F., Carlyle, J., McPherson, S., Thomas, R., Pasco Fearon, R., Goldberg, D., & Taylor, D. (2015). Pragmatic randomized controlled trial of long-term psychoanalytic psychotherapy for treatment-resistant depression: The Tavistock Adult Depression Study (TADS). *World Psychiatry, 14*(3), 312–321.

Freud, S. (1916/1917). *Mourning and Melancholy (Collected Works)*. Vol. XII, p. 428. Frankfurt a.M.: Fischer.

Gibbons, M. B. C., Gallop, R., Thompson, D., Luther, D., Crits-Christoph, K., Jacobs, J., Yin, S., & Crits-Christoph, P. (2016). Comparing effectiveness of cognitive therapy and dynamic psychotherapy for major depressive disorder in a community mental health setting. A randomized clinical noninferiority trial. *JAMA Psychiatry, 73*, 904–911.

Gold, P. W., Machado-Vieira, R., & Pavlatou, M. G. (2015). Clinical and biochemical manifestations of depression: Relation to the neurobiology of stress. *Neural Plasticity, 2015*, 581976. http://dx.doi.org/10.1155/2015/581976

Hengartner, M. P. (2019). Scientific debate instead of beef, challenging misleading arguments about the efficacy of antidepressants. *Acta Neuropsychiatrica, 31*(4), 235–236.

Hölzel, L., Härter, M., Reese, C., & Kriston, L. (2011). Risk factors for chronic depression–a systematic review. *Journal of Affective Disorders, 129*(1–3), 1–13.

Huber, D., & Klug, G. (2016). Munich psychotherapy study. *Psychotherapist, 61*(6), 462–467.

Huhn, M., Tardy, M., Spineli, L. M., Kissling, W., Förstl, H., Pitschel-Walz, G., Leucht, C., Samara, M., Dold, M., Davis, J.M., & Leucht, S. (2014). Efficacy of pharmacotherapy and psychotherapy for adult psychiatric disorders: A systematic overview of meta-analyses. *JAMA Psychiatry, 71*(6), 706–715. https://doi.org/10.1001/jamapsychiatry.2014.112

Knekt, P., Lindfors, O., Laaksonen, M. A., Renlund, C., Haaramo, P., Härkänen, T., & Helsinki (2011). Psychotherapy Study Group. Quasi-experimental study on the effectiveness of psychoanalysis, long-term and short-term psychotherapy on psychiatric symptoms, work ability and functional capacity during a 5-year follow-up. *Journal of Affective Disorders, 13*, 37–47.

Krakau, L., Ernst, M., Hautzinger, M., Beutel, M., & Leuzinger-Bohleber, M. (2023). Long-term psychotherapy of chronic depression and early trauma: Differential benefits of psychoanalytic compared to cognitive behavioral treatments. Submitted to *World Psychiatry*.

Küchenhoff, J. (2010). Zum Verhältnis von Psychopharmakologie und Psychoanalyse–am Beispiel der Depressionsbehandlung. *Psyche—Z Psychoanal, 64*(9–10), 890–916.

Leichsenring, F., Biskup, J., Kreische, R., & Staats, H. (2005). The Göttingen study of psychoanalytic therapy: First results. *The International Journal of Psychoanalysis, 6*(2), 433–455.

Leichsenring, F. (2008). Effectiveness of long-term psychodynamic psychotherapy. *JAMA, 300*(13), 1551–65.

Leichsenring, F., & Rabung, S. (2011). Long-term psychodynamic psychotherapy in complex mental disorders: Update of a meta-analysis. *British Journal of Psychiatry, 199*, 15–22.

Leichsenring, F., Luyten, P., Abbass, A., & Steinert, C. (2021a). Psychodynamic therapy of depression. *Australian & New Zealand Journal of Psychiatry*, *55*(12), 1202–1203.

Leichsenring, F., Luyten, P., Abbass, A., Rabung, S., & Steinert, C. (2021b).
Treatment of depression in children and adolescents. *The Lancet Psychiatry*,
8(2), 96–97.

Leuzinger-Bohleber, M. (2021). Contemporary psychodynamic theories on
depression. In J. P. Jiménez, A. Botto & P. Fonagy (Eds.), *Etiopathogenic
Theories and Models in Depression* (pp. 91–112). Cham, Switzerland:
Springer.

Leuzinger-Bohleber, M., Ambresin, G., Fischmann, T., & Solms, M. (Eds.)
(2022). *On the Dark Side. Understanding the Subjective Experience of Patients With Chronic Depression: Psychoanalytic, Neurobiological and Sociocultural Perspectives.* London: Routledge.

Leuzinger-Bohleber, M., Arnold, S., & Kächele, H. (Eds.) (2015/2019). *An
Open Door Review of Outcome and Process Studies in Psychoanalysis* (3rd
ed). IPA Website.

Leuzinger-Bohleber, M., Fischmann, T., & Beutel, M. E. (2022). *Chronische
Depression. Psychoanalytische Langzeittherapie*. Reihe: Praxis der psychodynamischen Psychotherapie—analytische und tiefenpsychologisch fundierte Psychotherapie, Bd. 12. Göttingen: Hogrefe Verlag.

Leuzinger-Bohleber, M., Grabhorn, A., & Bahrke, U. (2020). *Was nur erzählt,
und nciht gemessen werden kann. Einblicke in psychoanalytische Langzeitbehandlungen chronischer Depressionen* (What can only be told and not
measured. Insights into long-term psychoanalytic treatments of chronic depressed patients). Gießen: Psychosozial-Verlag.

Leuzinger-Bohleber, M., Hautzinger, M., Fiedler, G., Keller, W., Bahrke, U.,
Kallenbach, L., & Küchenhoff, H. (2019a). Outcome of psychoanalytic and
cognitive-behavioural long-term therapy with chronically depressed patients: A controlled trial with preferential and randomized allocation. *The
Canadian Journal of Psychiatry*, *64*(1), 47–58.

Leuzinger-Bohleber, M., Kaufhold, J., Kallenbach, L., Negele, A., Ernst, M.,
Keller, W., & Beutel, M. (2019b). How to measure sustained psychic transformations in long-term treatments of chronically depressed patients: Symptomatic and structural changes in the LAC depression study of the outcome
of cognitive-behavioral and psychoanalytic long-term treatments. *The International Journal of Psychoanalysis*, *100*(1), 99–127.

Leuzinger-Bohleber, M., Solms, M., & Arnold, S. E. (Eds.) (2020). *Outcome
Research and the Future of Psychoanalysis. Clinicians and Researchers in
Dialogue.* London: Routledge.

Leuzinger-Bohleber, M., Stuhr, U., Rüger, B., & Beutel, M. (2003). How to
study the 'quality of psychoanalytic treatments' and their long-term effects
on patients' well-being: A representative, multi-perspective follow-up study.
The International Journal of Psychoanalysis, *84*(2), 263–290.

Malhi, G. S., & Mann, J. J. (2018). Depression. *Lancet, 392*(10161), 2299–2312. https://doi.org/10.1016/s0140-6736(18)31948-2

Milton, J. (2001). Psychoanalysis and cognitive behavior therapy-rival paradigms or common ground? *International Journal of Psychoanalysis, 82*, 431–447.

Moussavi, S., Chatterji, S., Verdes, E., Tandon, A., Patel, V., & Ustun, B. (2007). Depression, chronic diseases, and decrements in health: Results from the world health surveys. *The Lancet, 370*, 851–858.

Munkholm, K., Paludan-Müller, A. S., & Boesen, K. (2019). Considering the methodological limitations in the evidence base of antidepressants for depression: A reanalysis of a network meta-analysis. *BMJ Open, 9*(6), e024886.

Nationale Leitlinie Unipolare Depression (NLV). (verabschiedet 29.2.2022), https://www.awmf.org/uploads/tx_szleitlinien/nvl-0051_S3_Unipolare_Depression_2022-10.pdf

Negele, A., Kaufhold, J., Kallenbach, L., & Leuzinger-Bohleber, M. (2015). Childhood trauma and its relation to chronic depression in adulthood. *Depression Research and Treatment, 2015*, 650804.

Rabung, S., & Leichsenring, F. (2016). Evidenz für psychodynamische Langzeittherapie. *Psychotherapeut, 61*, 441–446.

Rudolf, G., Jakobsen, T., Keller, W., Krawietz, B., Langer, M., Oberbracht, C., & Grande, T. (2012). Restructuring as an outcome paradigm of psychodynamic psychotherapy-results from the practice study analytic long-term therapy. *Journal of Psychosomatic Medicine and Psychotherapy, 58*(1), 55–66.

S3 *National Health Care Guidelines [NVL] Unipolar Depression.* (2022). (https://www.leitlinien.de/nvl/html/depression/kaptitel-2).

Schiele, S., & Kallenbach-Kaminski, L. (unpublished manuscript). *The role of parallel psychopharmacotherapy in the psychotherapeutic treatment of chronic depression.*

Schramm, E., Kriston, L., Zobel, I., Bailer, J., Wambach, K., Backenstrass, M., Klein, J. P., Schoepf, D., Schnell, K., Gumz, A., Bausch, P., Fangmeier, T., Meister, R., Berger, M., Hautzinger, M., & Härter, M. (2017). Effect of disorder-specific vs nonspecific psychotherapy for chronic depression. A randomized clinical trial. *JAMA Psychiatry, 74*, 233–242.

Springsteen, B. (2016). *Born to Run.* New York: Simon & Schuster.

Steinert, C., Hofmann, M., Kruse, J., & Leichsenring, F. (2014). Relapse rates after psychotherapy for depression—Stable long-term effects? A meta-analysis. *Journal of Affective Disorders, 168*, 107–118.

Steinert, C., Munder, T., Rabung, S., Hoyer, J., & Leichsenring, F. (2017). Psychodynamic therapy: As efficacious as other empirically supported treatments? A meta-analysis testing equivalence of outcomes. *American Journal of Psychiatry, 174*(10), 943–953.

Course of depressive symptoms in men and women: Differential effects of social, psychological, behavioral and somatic predictors. *Scientific Reports, 9*(1), 1–10. https://doi.org/10.1038/s41598-019-55342-0

Tibubos, A. N., Burghardt, J., Klein, E. M., Brähler, E., Jünger, C., Michal, M., Wiltink, J., Wild, P. S., Münzel, T., Singer, S., Pfeiffer, N., & Beutel, M. E. (2020). Frequency of stressful life events and associations with mental health and general subjective health in the general population. *Journal of Public Health, 29,* 1071–1080. https://doi.org/10.1007/s10389-020-01204-3

Trivedi, R. B., Nieuwsma, J. A., & Williams, J. W. Jr. (2011). Examination of the utility of psychotherapy for patients with treatment-resistant depression: A systematic review. *Journal of General Internal Medicine, 26,* 643–650.

Will, H., Grabenstedt, Y., Banck, G., & Volkl, G. (2008). *Depression: Psychodynamics and Therapy.* Kohlhammer Publishers.

World Health Organization. (2006). *The ICD-10 classification of mental and behavioural disorders* and WHO (2006), can be downloaded in the internet.

Chapter 2

Depression as a signature of our time

Although depressions have always been part of human reaction patterns, they have increased in recent years to such an extent that they have become a *signature of our time* in the social sciences. The phenomena of dissolution of boundaries and the enormous increase in individual choices of life perspectives lead to a loss of social security and make one's own identity a lifelong project of the individual. In his study, French sociologist Alain Ehrenberg (2016) declares the exhausted self to be the disease of contemporary society, whose norms of behavior are no longer based on guilt and discipline, but above all on responsibility and initiative. The late bourgeois individual seems to be replaced by an individual who has the idea that "everything is possible" and is characterized by anxiety about his or her self-actualization, which can easily increase to a feeling of exhaustion. The pressure to individualize is reflected in feelings of failure, shame, and inadequacy, and eventually in depressive symptoms. For Ehrenberg, neurosis is the disease of the individual torn by the conflict between what is permitted and what is forbidden. Depression, on the other hand, he describes as the disease of the individual who is inhibited and exhausted by the tension between the possible and the impossible. Depression thus becomes a tragedy of inadequacy (on the role of social and cultural factors in depression, see also Jiménez, Botto & Fonagy, 2021).

Ehrenberg's theses have triggered interesting debates especially in psychoanalytic social psychology, but also among historians and social scientists. Due to the pandemic, the climate catastrophe, and the worldwide refugee movements, also caused by wars and the clash of different ideologies and value systems (let's think, for example, of Putin's official legitimation of his attack on Ukraine, the current situation in Iran, or the propaganda of the Hamas), today for many people, not

DOI: 10.4324/9781003455349-2

mainly shame and inadequacy, but powerlessness, helplessness, and insecurity are in the center of their depressive illness, which should also be reflected in relation to the contemporary societal situation in Western democracies.

As I have put up for discussion in various papers on the pandemic (e.g., in Leuzinger-Bohleber & Blass, 2021; Leuzinger-Bohleber & Montigny, 2021), from a psychoanalytic point of view it can be assumed that some disturbing social processes, such as the worldwide increase in populism, fundamentalism, nationalism, and autocratic systems of rule, among others, are to be seen in connection with the individual and collective (omnipotent) defense against such unbearable feelings (cf., among others, Moser, 2013). Powerlessness and helplessness combined with a diffuse fear of death and an existential feeling of threat favor regressive processes into early narcissistic states in individuals but especially in groups and large groups, which can stimulate, for example, a longing for security in the bosom of the homeland, the nation.

Bohleber (2010/2012) most notably pointed toward the significance of narcissistic crises which predispose individuals, groups, and whole societies to fundamentalist (in fact Christian as well as Islamist) ideologies due to the fact that during such labile psychosocial crises ubiquitous unconscious fantasies are reactivated and narcissistic depletions of the self are being defended against by fantasies of grandiosity.

Referring to fundamentalist, nationalist, anti-Semitic, and Islamist ideologies, he primarily delineates three unconscious systems of fantasies. They are ubiquitous, meaning they exist in every person's unconscious. In the sense of "embodied memories" (Leuzinger-Bohleber, 2015, 2021, 2022) early and earliest, biologically determined experiences with our primary objects, before anything else the experience of extreme dependence, powerlessness, and fear of death on the one hand and seemingly paradisiac senses of pleasure on the other hand, remain in place and can therefore be mobilized within all of us in certain societal and individual constellations.

From a psychoanalytical perspective, it can be assumed that some social phenomena, such as the global rise in populism, fundamentalism, nationalism, and autocratic systems of rule, can be seen in connection with the individual and collective defense against the unbearable feelings outlined above. Powerlessness and helplessness combined with a diffuse fear of death and an existential feeling of threat promote regressive processes in early narcissistic states in individuals but above all in groups and large groups, which can, for example, stimulate a longing for security in the bosom of the homeland, the nation. In these regressive states, unconscious early fantasy systems resurface, such as the fantasy of merging with the omnipotent primary object that solves all problems, as well as the fantasy of "homogeneity and purity," in which a fantasized affiliation to a "pure," "homogeneous" group (such as "the Germans," "the Americans," and "the Russians") is associated with safety and security. Foreigners, "others" are experienced as intruders who pollute and destroy the fantasized unity or even, in the sense of early sibling envy, are unconsciously perceived as voracious parasites and a threat to prosperity and provision. All over the world, populist and fundamentalist politicians are masterfully playing the keyboard of such unconscious fantasies. In diffuse life-threatening situations during individual and social crises, they succeed in mobilizing them in many people and abusing them for their own purposes.

As will be discussed below, this social danger exists not only because it is a defense against depression but also because the painful psychological wounds of trauma can be made to disappear from the consciousness of those affected.

References

Bohleber, W. (2010). *Was Psychoanalyse heute leistet. Identität und Intersubjektivität, Trauma und Therapie, Gewalt und Gesellschaft.* Stuttgart: Klett-Cotta. In English (not identical publication): Bohleber, W. (2012). *Destructiveness, Intersubjectivity, and Trauma: The Identity Crisis of Modern Psychoanalysis.* London: Karnac.

Ehrenberg, A. (2016). *The Weariness of the Self: Diagnosing the History of Depression in the Contemporary Age.* Montreal, Quebec, McGill-Queen's Press-MQUP.

Jiménez, J. P., Botto, A., & Fonagy, P. (Eds.). (2021). *Depression and Personality. Etiopathogenic Theories and Models in Depression.* Cham, Switzerland: Springer.

Leuzinger-Bohleber, M. (2015). *Finding the Body in the Mind—Embodied Memories, Trauma, and Depression.* International Psychoanalytical Association, London: Karnac.

Leuzinger-Bohleber, M. (2021). Contemporary psychodynamic theories on depression. In J. P. Jiménez, A. Botto & P. Fonagy (Eds.), *Etiopathogenic Theories and Models in Depression* (pp. 91–112). Cham, Switzerland: Springer.

Leuzinger-Bohleber, M. (2022). "... I feel very alien and forever alien in this world..." (Susan Taubes). Depression—An illness of ideals and trauma.

Paper given at the EPF Conference in Vienna, July 16, 2022 (is published in the *EPF Bulletin* in German, English and French, 2022).

Leuzinger-Bohleber, M., & Blass, H. (Eds.). (2021). Special issue: Psycho-analytic contributions to understanding the COVID-19 pandemic. *International Journal of Applied Psychoanalytic Studies, 18*(2), 107–241. https://onlinelibrary.wiley.com/toc/15569187/2021/18/2

Leuzinger-Bohleber, M., & Montigny, N. (2021). The pandemic as a develop-mental risk. *International Journal of Applied Psychoanalytic Studies, 18*(2), 121–132. https://doi.org/10.1002/aps.1706

Moser, U. (2013). *Theorie der Abwehrprozesse: Die Mentale Organisation Psychischer Störungen*. Brandes & Apsel Verlag.

Chapter 3

Depression and trauma

Long a neglected topic in both clinical and extra-clinical psychoanalytic research[1]

3.1 Clinical and conceptual research on depression in psychoanalysis

3.1.1 Depression in response to loss: Guilt depression and reparation

In contemporary and "classical" psychoanalysis, depression is seen as a reaction to the loss of a real object in the patient's external reality or/ and a loss of an inner object, an inner relationship or one's own object and self-ideal representations. However, the focus of psychoanalytic understanding is not so much the object loss itself, but its psychic processing. In *Mourning and Melancholy* (Freud, 1916/1917), Sigmund Freud distinguishes between mourning and melancholy. Grief is an "out-of-tune" feeling with a painful mood, a withdrawal of interest in the outside world, a loss of the ability to love, and an inhibition of creativity in work and leisure. All this serves to surrender to the grief and to facilitate the mourning process. The grieving individual painfully works through his memories of the lost object in order to be able to withdraw the libidinal cathexis from the object and finally accept the loss. If the withdrawal of libido from the object is successful, then the mourning comes to an end. The ego is "free and uninhibited again." Metaphorically speaking, the libido can now look around for other objects.

The pathological grief in melancholia arises from a deep ambivalence toward the object, as well as from narcissistic wounds and experienced disappointments in the relationship with the object. Unlike normal grief, the object is not abandoned psychically. The attachment is maintained by incorporating the object into the ego through

DOI: 10.4324/9781003455349-3

narcissistic identification. Now the ego, or one's own self, feels the hatred that was originally directed at the object: as a result, one's own ego is attacked, devalued, and humiliated instead of the object.

The inner object relations are thereby regressed to the level of infantile sadism. At the same time, the process of identification and incorporation establishes a "critical voice" in the ego. The object selected according to the narcissistic type subsequently assumes the role of a judge as an (unconscious) part of the ego: the accusations against the object become self-reproaches.

In *The Ego and the Id* (1923/2000), Freud recognized that the processes of introjection and primary identification play a central role not only in melancholia but are important mechanisms in early development more generally. The replacement of the cathexis of the object by identification becomes a constituent condition of the subject. The character of the ego is formed through the "lasting traces of the old object relations." Freud thus also revised his strict separation between grief and melancholy, for early object relations always shape the personality structure of the ego thanks to the ongoing identifications with them. Accordingly, the attachment to the lost object is not simply abandoned but transformed in a restructuring process, which allows the memories to become a permanent part of the inner world (Hagmann, 1995). With the structural theory and his insights into the influence of the superego, Freud can better grasp the conflicts and tensions between the superego and the ego. The overpowering superego fills the consciousness of the depressed person and rages against the ego. It has seized sadistic impulses of the individual and turned them destructively against the ego. Freud now calls this psychic constellation prevailing in the superego a "pure culture of the death drive," which often enough succeeds in actually driving the ego to its death.

Karl Abraham had already identified hatred as a cause of depression in 1911 (Abraham, 1911), leading to repressed self-reproach and guilt. Like Freud, he also recognized identification as a fundamental mechanism in 1924 (Abraham, 1924). If a person prone to depression loses his or her love object, he or she reacts with hatred and contempt, the frustrating object is expelled and, in the course of a regression to the oral-sadistic stage, is finally incorporated right back into the self. Through this narcissistic identification with the devalued, hated object, the self itself becomes worthless and reacts melancholically.

This psychodynamic understanding of depression described by Freud and Abraham has been taken up by various psychoanalytic researchers. According to it, the decisive determinant for the outbreak of depression is, as already mentioned, not the loss of the real object itself, but a pre-existing strongly marked ambivalence or aggression. The already existing ambivalences, which have their origin in narcissistic injuries by the object, are additionally intensified after its loss.

Sándor Radó, Melanie Klein, and Edith Jacobson also described in their works the sadistic aggressiveness of the superego as an important factor of depression. In Melanie Klein's work, the archaic severity of the early superego results from the splitting of the object and self-representations into an "ideal good object" on the one hand and a "fantasized evil" on the other. Through the later integration of these split-off parts into the self-representations, the child becomes aware of his own aggression against the idealized primary object and falls into depression. Melanie Klein introduces the concept of reparation in the so-called depressive position. In the depressive position, the subject manages to integrate libidinous and aggressive impulses, thoughts, and drives and to undergo processes of reparation. When excessive aggressive impulses dominate the libidinous ones, such integration and reparation cannot take place: depression results.[2]

Edith Jacobson (1971) describes a basic conflict found in all depressive states. When the ego cannot achieve the satisfaction it desires and cannot use its aggression to achieve that satisfaction, it turns the aggressive impulses against its self-representation. A narcissistic conflict arises between the desired self-image and the image of the failing devalued real self. Self-esteem is lost: a depressive mood develops. Severe depression is found primarily in people whose early frustrations and injuries had a devastating effect on psychic development because they were associated with unusual hostility on the part of their primary objects. Early frustrations produce exaggerated expectations, love objects are idealized. Ego ideals and wishful self-conceptions are exaggerated and unattainable. New narcissistic wounds lead to a devaluation of the love object. In order to endure and make up for these wounds, glorified fantasies of grandiosity of the love objects are introjected into the superego, whereas the devalued fantasies of a bad parent are introjected into the ego. Thus the child can hold on to the hope of love in the future, but from now on is exposed to the massive criticism and hostility of his own idealized unconscious fantasies and evaluations. At the same time, the narcissistic self-regulation of the ego is permanently damaged (see also Kernberg, 2009).

3.1.2   Narcissistic and psychotic depression

Psychoanalytic authors have repeatedly addressed the fact that in depressed patients the ego or self is particularly vulnerable and intolerant of frustration and disappointment. It also seems that self and object representations are not yet sufficiently differentiated from each other. As early as 1928, Sándor Radó noted the special tendency of depressed patients to passive-dependent object relations because this was the only way they could maintain their self-esteem. This is followed by a somewhat different basic understanding of basic depressive conflicts. Radó (1928) sees the basic disorder in the context of narcissistic self-regulation and describes it as the tension between strongly expressed narcissistic expectations and ideals on the one hand and the inability to live up to these ideals while being supported by benevolent objects on the other. One result of this is depressive affect.

In 1953, Eduard Bibring was the first to elaborate on this explanatory approach, distinguishing it from the assumption of aggression directed at the self as the main determinant of depression. For him, depression is primarily an emotional expression of a state of helplessness of the self. They correspond to general human experiences. The self is often in a state of real or imagined helplessness in the face of overwhelming difficulties.

Other authors speak of *narcissistic depression in* view of the underlying tensions between ego and ego-ideal. Here, it is not feelings of guilt nourished by aggression and self-hatred that dominate, but shame and humiliation, as well as feelings of abandonment and helplessness. Joffe and Sandler (1965) describe the loss of narcissistic integrity as the central cause of the depressive reaction. The focus is not so much on the loss of a love object but on the loss of one's own well-being, which is inextricably linked to it. It is the feeling of having been deprived of an ideal psychic state. If the individual feels helpless, resigned in the face of the emotional pain experienced, and cannot find relief by aggression directed to objects in the outside world, he or she reacts affectively with depression.

Wolfgang Loch (Loch & Kutter, 1967) also assumes an imbalance between the individual's ideals and his self-esteem. The perception of this discrepancy produces a depressive affect. In the depressed patient, there is no stable connection between the self and the ideal self because the process of identification of the self with the ideal object is disturbed by aggressive impulses and fantasies. Therefore, the connection between the self and the ideal self is guaranteed only as long as the real presence of an ideal object is present. If the external object is lost, the subject is exposed to his inner ambivalence: depression is a consequence of this process.

In *psychotic depression,* the ideal self is lost, forcing the cathexis of the superego as a substitute. This archaic persecutory superego has taken over the function of the ego and deprives the depressive of his self-esteem: a realistic, positive self-assessment is lost. If the libidinous cathexis of the ideal object was already disturbed in early childhood, a depressive feeling of emptiness and a massive inhibition of one's own vitality may develop later in life.

3.1.3 Integrative models of depression

Another group of psychoanalysts does not try to describe a single, central basic conflict, but to develop an integrative model of depressive states of mind in view of the diversity of pathogenic conflict constellations in depression (Bohleber, 2005; Blatt & Zuroff, 2005). Stavros Mentzos (1995) assumes narcissistic self-regulation supported by a mature ideal-self, ideal-object, and superego in a mature self-regulation. A blockage or pathological development of one of these factors of self-regulation leads to various clinical pictures of depression (e.g., mania, anaclitic depression, and guilt depression). Herbert Will (1994) classifies different forms of depression according to different guiding emotions: superego or guilt depression with guilt and self-accusation; oral-dependent depression with anxious longing and disappointment; ego depression with helplessness and hopelessness; narcissistic depression with shame and self-deprecations.

Based on many empirical studies, Sidney J. Blatt (2004) characterized two different organizations of depression: the anaclitic type, which focuses on interpersonal factors such as dependence, helplessness, feelings of loss, and abandonment. In contrast, the introjective type exhibits a strict, punitive superego, self-criticism, low self-esteem, and basal feelings of failure and guilt.

Bleichmar (1996) attributes a central role in the onset of depression to feelings of helplessness and hopelessness. In the predepressed individual, there is a fixation on a desire that takes a central position in the libidinous economy of the subject. Therefore, a lost object cannot be replaced by any other. The fulfillment of one's desires seems unattainable, leading to a sense of deep helplessness and a self-representation of powerlessness. A feeling of hopelessness spreads, extending not only to the present but also to the future. All this leads to successively fewer attempts to fulfill one's own drive desires at all: depressive moods, apathy, and psychomotor inhibitions are the consequences.

As shown in the following graph, there are quite different pathways that psychodynamically cause and determine a depressive state. None is obligatory, each is determined by different factors and psychodynamic constellations.

As discussed above, most authors give aggression a prominent or even universal place in the psychodynamics of depression (see dynamics in the upper left part of Figure 3.1). In addition, Bleichmar (1996) lists the following factors: guilt and blame; frustration in achieving narcissistic aspirations; narcissistic personality disorder (either with weak narcissistic self-regulation or with traits of grandiosity and omnipotence that collapse when confronted with reality) (dynamics on the upper right side of Figure 3.1); persecutory anxiety; ego deficits; traumatic experiences. These factors can operate individually, but also in combination or sequentially, as Bleichmar illustrates in three extended case examples (for more details, see Bleichmar, 1996).

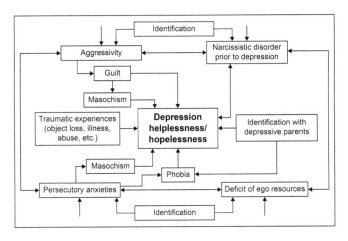

Figure 3.1 Pathways of depression development according to Hugo Bleichmar (2010).

3.2   Chronic depression, trauma, and embodied memories and their transgenerational transmission[3]

As mentioned above, severe trauma is very common in chronically depressed patients. Therefore, in the following, we will deal with the treatment considerations that result from this. In our clinical experience, however, these considerations also apply to psychoanalytic depression treatment in general.

The extreme feeling of helplessness and hopelessness is not only a central basic feeling of depression as discussed above, but also characterizes traumatic experiences. In the psychoanalytic literature, an adequate understanding of trauma continues to be struggled with to this day. Cooper (1986), for example, referred to Freud when he defined:

> Psychological trauma is an event that abruptly overwhelms the ego's ability to provide for a minimal sense of security and integrative completeness, resulting in overwhelming fear or helplessness or the threat thereof, and it causes a permanent change in psychological organization.
>
> (p. 44) (see also chapter 1)

For Freud, too, it was the effects of extreme stimulus overload of the ego in wartime situations that motivated him to conceptualize trauma and its consequences: he had originally observed them in war neuroses during World War I: the natural protection against stimuli is broken by a sudden, unanticipated extreme experience, usually associated with threat to life and fear of death. The ego is exposed to a feeling of extreme powerlessness and inability to control or cope with the situation and is flooded with panic and extreme physiological reactions. This flooding of the ego results in a state of psychological and physiological shock. The traumatic experience destroys the empathic shield provided by the internalized primary object and destroys confidence in the continued presence of good objects and the expectability of human empathy. In trauma, the inner good object falls silent as an empathic mediator between self and environment (cf. also Bohleber, 2010/2012).

Psychoanalytic knowledge of short- and long-term effects of severe traumatization comes primarily from clinical work with survivors of the Shoah and their children and infants (see, among others,

Grubrich-Simitis, 1979; Keilson, 1979; Faimberg, 1987; Krystal, 1988; Cournut, 1988; Keilson, et al., 1992; Abraham & Torok, 1994; Kogan, 1995; Auerhahn & Laub, 1998). What the victims of the Shoah experienced is beyond all of us to imagine. The incomprehensible nature of trauma can only be described in psychoanalytic-scientific terms such as "massive psychic trauma" (cf., e.g., Krystal, 1988), sequential (Keilson, 1979; Keilson, et al., 1992), or cumulative traumatization (Khan, 1964) only in a rough approximation.

The survivors of such extreme traumatizations showed that such extreme traumatizations cannot be psychically processed, but lead to lifelong consequences, which, however, can take very different, individual forms (nightmares, flashbacks, loneliness and depression, experiences of dissociation and derealization, disturbances in the sense of time and identity, diffuse panic, anxiety and attacks of aggression, emotional encapsulation, a breakdown of a primal trust in the protective, good object and basal structures of meaning in life, as well as psychosomatic disorders such as sleep disturbances, pain states that cannot be localized, etc.). The deep psychic wounds associated with this can at most be alleviated even in long psychoanalyses, but never really "healed." Moreover, the experienced trauma is often transferred to the second and third generations (see also, e.g., Leuzinger-Bohleber, 2003). For understandable reasons, it took almost 60 years until psychoanalysts in Germany started to also talk about the effects of severe traumatization in the families of the persecuted and fellow travelers during the time of National Socialism. The concern to equate the unimaginable, what the victims of the Shoah had experienced, with the suffering in families, which had been actively involved in the National Socialist crimes, is still justified.

It was, among other things, an unexpected result of the Follow-Up study of the German Psychoanalytic Association (DPV) that drew professional attention to the long-term consequences of traumatic experiences of the German population during World War II: 62% of the 402 patients who had sought help in psychoanalyses or psychoanalytic long-term therapies in the 1980s were traumatized former war children (see, e.g., Leuzinger-Bohleber, 2003; Radebold, Heuft & Fooken, 2006). As noted above, also among the unexpected findings of the LAC depression study was that 84% of chronically depressed patents had suffered severe childhood trauma.

Other clinical and empirical studies also demonstrated the short- and long-term consequences of trauma caused by so-called "man-made disasters." Thus, it is now undisputed that traumatic experiences lead to a great vulnerability of the traumatized even after overcoming the acute danger (see, among others, Leuzinger-Bohleber et al., 2003; Bohleber, 2010/2012; see also, for example, Gaensbauer, 1995, 2011; Laub, 2005; Hauser, 2008; Gabbard, 2018), which manifests itself in all their relationships and, of course, on psychotherapeutic treatment. Therefore, traumatization and its transgenerational consequences have to be taken into account in their treatment techniques, because especially psychoanalysts in Germany, but also in other European countries, still treat many traumatized patients suffering from the long (often unconscious) shadows of the catastrophes of World War II and National Socialism on the second and third generations.

As Bohleber and Leuzinger-Bohleber (2016) discuss: in many cases, traumatic experiences can only be remembered in fragments because they are disconnected from current consciousness. In psychoanalyses or psychoanalytic therapy, the patient unconsciously repeats the traumatic experiences e.g. in enactments or specific transference fantasies. As will be briefly outlined, these clinical phenomena can be used as a key to understanding early traumatization (see also Leuzinger-Bohleber, 2015a, 2021).

Since Freud, generations of psychoanalysts have dealt with how unprocessed, unconscious conflicts of the past determine the present, can be repeated in the transference, and successively transferred into a healing memory process. For the most part, this involved symbolically represented and repressed memories or patterns of relationships. But, as just outlined, especially severe early traumatizations are often characterized by the fact that they elude symbolization and mentalization. Therefore, the theory and clinic of psychoanalysis have for some years been concerned with psychic material that is present in other ways in the analytic relationship. *Unrepresented States and the Construction of Meaning is what* Levine, Reed and Scarfone (2013) call their anthology, which they dedicate to André Green and focus on this question of making sense of the unrepresented from a contemporary perspective. Green (2007) has described with his widely received concept of the "dead mother" that early separations from the primary object that cannot be processed lead to an identification with this object, to a withdrawal of cathexis, and thus to a disappearance of the inner representations, which can be perceived in the transference relationship by the analyst as a void, a negative hallucination of the object, "a representation of the absence of representation" (Green,

1993, p. 196, cited in Reed, 2013, p. 39). Reed (2013, p. 29ff.) points out that the negative hallucination of the object—*an empty mirror*—is basically always there in these patients, but often only becomes observable in the analysand's extreme reactions to separations from the analyst.

Green was concerned with the process of disobjectalization, that is, the erasure of representations. Other psychoanalytic researchers, on the other hand, focused on the psychic material of patients that has insufficiently or never undergone a process of symbolization, as seen in some severely traumatized individuals. Dominique Scarfone (2013) presents a conceptual integration of different forms of psychic representation and their different psychoanalytic conceptualizations. He compares Pierce's theory of signs with Freud's notion of primary and secondary process, with Lacan's theory of the real, the imaginary, and the symbolic, with Bion's beta and alpha elements, with Laplanche's infantile sexual theories and their decoding in analytic discourse, and with Piera Aulagnier's concept of the "primary," such as "primary violence" that is staged (mise en scène) and can eventually be revealed to secondary-process discourse: a brilliant example of contemporary psychoanalytic conceptual research.

Leuzinger-Bohleber and Pfeifer (2002) took a different approach to conceptualizing the effects of early, unsymbolized traumatic experiences. They referred to studies from the field of basic sciences, specifically Embodied Cognitive Science and cognitive neuroscience, to show that these disciplines offer *initial explanatory models for,* among other things, *the* clinically important phenomenon of how spontaneous ideas of the analyst—for example, in an initial scene in the first interview—emerge and can constitute a first, crucial step toward understanding previously unrepresented mental material, especially in traumatized patients, and making it accessible to psychoanalytic processing.[4]

Inspired by biology and the life sciences, Embodied Cognitive Science now understands memory not as the retrieval of knowledge statically stored in the brain, but as a function of the whole organism, which is the product of complex, dynamic recategorization and interactive processes that are always "embodied" (see also Gallese, 2013a, 2013b).

Memories of past (traumatic) situations are known to unconsciously determine present thinking, feeling, and acting, but not in the sense of stored knowledge in analogy to a computer or static memory traces. In contrast, memories are products of dynamic, complex constructions in the here and now. In the embodiment sense, sensorimotor coordinations in the present always function analogously to previous situations. The similarities between a present and a past situation are not perceived cognitively, for example, by cognitive pattern matching, but by similarly complex information obtained from different senses (auditory, visual, olfactory, touch, smell, etc.) and actions of the body. These processes are characterized in Embodied Cognitive Science as sensorimotor coordination. Through such sensorimotor coordination, memories and categories are automatically constructed as a self-regulatory process of learning by doing (John Dewey), that is, by coordinating information from sensory channels and connected (motor) actions of the body. Memories resulting from sensorimotor coordination thus provide orientation in a new situation and are always based on the subject's previous experiences.

Embodiment is therefore a perspective that always takes into account the developmental aspect (see, among others, Edelman, 1987, 1989; Damasio, 1994; Lakoff & Johnson, 1999; Leuzinger-Bohleber & Pfeifer, 2002; Green, 2007; Pfeifer & Bongard, 2007; Mizen, 2009; Leuzinger-Bohleber, 2015a[5]). In several papers, Leuzinger-Bohleber and Pfeifer (2002) illustrated that this understanding of unconscious embodied memories proves particularly fruitful for decoding early, pre-verbal traumatization in the therapeutic situation.

Briefly summarized: memories have often been explained in psychoanalysis using a representational model in which traumatic experiences are not psychically integrated due to excessive arousal, but are incompletely represented or not registered at all. After a radical rethinking that changes the understanding of memories and their relevance for transformation processes in psychoanalysis, alternative interdisciplinary conceptualizations of memory and remembering are now available. This new interdisciplinary knowledge has consequences for the treatment technique of chronically depressed, early traumatized patients who were so frequently treated in the Coomparative Outcome Study on Chronic Depressed Patients (LAC Study) (see Leuzinger-Bohleber, 2015a; Bohleber & Leuzinger-Bohleber, 2016).

In the manual "Chronic Depression," we draw on the conceptualizations just outlined and illustrate the resulting treatment considerations with concrete case examples (see Leuzinger-Bohleber, Fischmann & Beutel, 2022). In this volume, a short summary of a psychoanalysis in the frame of the **M**ultilevel **O**utcome Study of Psychoanalysis of

Chronically **De**pressed Patients with **E**arly Trauma (MODE) study (see Chapter 2). might illustrate the just mentioned transgenerational dimension of depression as well as the seismographic reaction of chronically depressed patients to societal trauma in the presence due to embodied memories of their own early trauma. In addition, some characteristic demands on the treatment technique with these seriously ill patients, such as the handling of their suicidality and extreme withdrawals, are illustrated. A few more remarks on this topic are given in the next section. For more details, I must refer to the treatment manual of the LAC and MODE studies (Leuzinger-Bohleber, Fischmann & Beutel, 2022).

3.3 Some remarks on specific challenges in psychoanalyses with chronically depressed patients with early trauma[6]

David Taylor (2010) shares Hugo Bleichmar's view (see Section 3.1) that depression can result from a variety of psychodynamic causes.

> Thus, the depressive reaction is a final common pathway, comparable to the constant reactions of an inflammatory response. The constant elements of which are usually not the actual cause of the pathology, but a universal protective reaction, which, however, can become excessive and then cause problems.
>
> (p. 854, translation MLB)

In the following section, we will briefly discuss some specific challenges related to these "inflammations" in psychoanalytic treatments of chronically depressed, early traumatized patients.[7]

3.3.1 Suicidality

Suicidality is one of the central symptoms of chronic depression. Therefore, this topic must be thoroughly clinically examined and discussed in the assessment interviews prior to treatment. If a psychoanalysis or a psychoanalytic long-term therapy is agreed, the psychoanalyst/therapist must openly discuss with the patient how suicidal thoughts will be dealt with during treatment (see below and Chapter 4).

Will (1994, p. 183) summarized the risk of suicide attempts and successful suicides as follows: the suicidal risk is increased if there is a history of one or more suicide attempts, if the suicide attempts were carried out by "hard" means (e.g., attempted hanging), if there is frequent and abusive use of medication, alcohol, or drugs, if the illness is chronic and is processed with resignation, and if there is an accumulation of suicide attempts or suicides in the family history.

All these topics should therefore be explored in the assessment interviews (cf. 4). In addition, it is particularly important in this context that psychoanalysts carefully observe their own countertransference reactions. Can he imagine dealing with the patient's suicidal impulses? Are these impulses expressed openly? Are they hidden or do they proceed mainly unconsciously? What is their intensity and quality? What do they trigger in the analyst himself? Do they touch on his own difficult unconscious constellations? Can he look with the patient into the abysses of suicidality, despair, contempt for life, murderous destruction, and longing for death?

It is known that the patient often only ventures into the abysses of his suicidal tendencies when he feels held and contained during treatment. Often chronically depressed persons have had the experience that earlier suicidal impulses (as a child or as an adolescent) were neither recognized nor emotionally tolerated by their close caregivers. Therefore, the affected persons remained alone with these abysses of their psyche. As many psychoanalyses of the LAC study showed the experience of being able to share these abysses with the psychoanalyst, to explore them together in order to deal with them in a reasonably creative way, was one of the most important therapeutic experiences of the affected patients. The emotional, holding relationship with the psychoanalyst is essential. Therefore, one of the most important personal indication criteria for this group of patients is whether the psychoanalyst can imagine establishing a sustainable, professional relationship with a particular patient, capable of professionally managing difficult treatment crises, often associated with suicidal impulses. If too many personal doubts arise in a therapist/analyst during the assessment as to whether he or she can assume such a holding role in treatment with a specific patient, he or she should not offer the patient treatment but refer him or her to another study therapist.

Different subgroups of suicidal fantasies in depressed patients have been distinguished. To mention only one of them here: Kind (1992) describes (a) a suicidal tendency that is in the service of symbiotic fusion desires with the primary object. A second group (b) Kind characterizes as "antifusionary" because these fantasies serve to ward off too intense longings for closeness to the object. Finally, (c) he speaks of a manipulative and resignative suicidal tendency borne of a desperate attempt to achieve emotional resonance in the object or to confirm the unconscious truth that the object is incapable of doing so and does not really care about the patient.

These different unconscious fantasies lead to different countertransference reactions of the analyst and to different emotional reactions to them.

It is to be hoped that in phases of treatment in which suicidal fantasies and impulses are latent or overt, the patient has identified himself in a "good enough" way with the basic rule of psychoanalysis, that is, that he will "free associate" in the sessions and pay attention to all fantasies, thoughts, emotions, and bodily reactions. Anything that can be thought, felt, and in some way communicated to the analyst minimizes the likelihood of translating suicidal fantasies and impulses into concrete action, in the sense of "enactment."

Therefore, many authors describe the importance of paying careful attention to the analyst's emotional withdrawals (see case example, Chapter 4). If the analyst does not reach the depressed patient emotionally for a long period of time during the sessions, this is often an alarm signal.

Some authors describe the so-called *presuicidal syndrome* (Ringel & Sonneck, 1978), which may occur in relation to the patient's overall life situation or in relation to the treatment itself. In this phase, the patient is inwardly constricted to suicidal ideation and feels relieved because he or she has made the decision to commit suicide. This subjective relief is sometimes mistakenly interpreted by therapists as improvement.

It is particularly dangerous when the patient is completely isolated socially, has no supportive object relationships, and is not integrated into stable everyday structures either professionally or personally. Will (1994) and Will et al. (2008) mention the following warning signs for analysts:

- The emotional confinement to the negative and hopeless experience,
- The increase of aggression to a powerless rage that can only be discharged on one's own self. Often it seems split off and hides behind a cool "standing above things,"

• The withdrawal from reality by escaping into a fantasy world associated with suicidal thoughts, for example, from a paradisiacal state after a suicide. (Will, 1994, p. 172/173).

Example 1: Suicidal fantasies related to the desire to merge with the object.

A dream of Mrs A which she told already in her first assessment interview (see Section 1.1 in Chapter 1), may illustrate the group of suicidal patients who unconsciously long for a fusion with the lost object. In her dream these passive death longings were clearly evident: "I am standing by the sea—a big, dark wave comes and pulls me out … I don't resist, but find it beautiful to surrender to it …" The psychoanalyst saw this as a warning sign of acute suicidal danger and therefore decided to offer the patient a low-frequency treatment in a vis-à-vis position. She agreed with the patient that she would have to call her any time she felt that she or her husband could no longer control their suicidal impulses. With this agreement, the psychoanalyst wanted to offer herself as a viable psychoanalytic object and prevent Mrs A from continuing an exclusive attachment to the psychiatrist who had treated her in the clinic in a problematic, unresolved transference relationship. She feared that, in the sense of a split, Mrs A would experience the psychiatrist as a "helping, viable object" and the psychoanalyst as an "uninterested, weak, emotionally neglectful object." In contrast, with this agreement, she stimulated the development of a transference to a "whole object" instead of a "partial object."

This arrangement proved to be productive in this individual case: thus, Mrs A brought her suicidal fantasies directly into the treatment and was able to talk about these fantasies instead of acting them out (e.g., tormenting the analyst with her phone calls at night).

Example 2: Antifusionary suicide fantasies

In contrast: Mr A's treating psychoanalyst had a completely different experience in the first confrontation with the suicidal impulses (see summary of the psychoanalysis with Mr A in

chapter 4). After the end of the first week of the high-frequency
psychoanalysis, Mr A sat down on the couch at the beginning of
the 4th analytic session, turned to the analyst, and said, "I have
to ask you a question: If I were really in distress, could I turn
to the senior physician at your institute and ask for help?" The
analyst immediately registered in her countertransference most
intense feelings of devaluation and attack on her psychoanalytic
potency. Although she tried to control her emotions, Mr A accurately perceived this, stood up, and said. "Then I will leave
now—I see that I have hurt you. I'm sure you don't want to
work with me now …"

Only many months later it became understandable that Mr A
had acted out part of an intense negative mother transference.
He was unconsciously convinced that the psychoanalyst, like his
alcoholic mother, could not and would not take care of him if
he ever really found himself in emotional or physical distress:
therefore, he preferred to break off the incipient relationship
right away and get to safety. As it turned out, this staging also
contained his suicidal impulses, which could be understood as
antifusionary: he preferred to break off an incipient relationship
to face the danger of relying on an object that could not emotionally care for and hold him but was absorbed by his own misery.

Moreover, some authors have warned that the psychoanalyst should
not be deceived by euphoric statements of the patient that he feels better, that the treatment is helpful, "he is over the hill, leave the shadow
valley behind." Among others, Böker (2011) pointed out that especially in moments when the patient can increasingly dispose of his
own life impulses, there is a danger that he will use this activity to
carry out a suicidal action.

3.3.2 Aggression and guilt and their significance for the end of treatment

As mentioned earlier, depression is often triggered by an experience
of loss.

Freud already described in "Mourning and Melancholia" that the es-
sence of the depressive phenomenon does not lie in the loss itself, but
in the way the loss is processed and with which unconscious fantasies

it is connected. Central to this is the fantasy that the object is not replaceable or cannot be replaced.

Thus, the quality of the inner relationship to the lost object plays a decisive role for these processes. If the relationship was characterized by strong ambivalence, pathological mourning is likely. The "shadow of the object falls on the ego." As Bleichmar (1996) states, it is important to

> differentiate between effects aggression produces when directed at the representation of the object or at the representation of the self, from the effects it produces when it is acted out against the real, external object or against its *functions* for the self (p. 940).

The fantasy of having damaged or even destroyed the object often leads to unbearable feelings of guilt and may even stimulate suicidal impulses: the subject does not deserve to continue living, but must follow the object to death.

Here is an example from a psychoanalytic crisis intervention with a severely traumatized refugee as part of the STEP-BY-STEP project.[8]

Mr L was presented to me during the weekly psychoanalytic consultation in Michaelisdorf (see, e.g., Leuzinger-Bohleber et al., 2016): he was in a desolate mental and physical state, had hardly eaten or slept for days: he just lay frozen, in a kind of state of shock, in his bed in the dark. He was acutely suicidal.

Having succeeded in entering into an inner, emotionally resonant relationship with him, I was flooded with panic, despair, fear of death, and helplessness in my countertransference. Finally, after a long pause, I say:

> "I have a feeling that you are not well at all. Would you like to tell me something about it?"—"I have terrible dreams every night, so that I dare not go to sleep …"—"Perhaps it would be good if you could tell me such a dream …" After a short silence: "Last night I fell asleep for a moment. Then I dreamed that I was standing at the open grave of my father in Afghanistan. Then suddenly the corpse reached out to me and wanted to pull me down to the grave … I woke up in a panic …"

Mr L then hesitantly tells me that his father and one of his brothers were killed by the Taliban because they belonged to an ethnic minority. He was also captured and tortured, but managed to escape … It becomes clear that he suffers from unbearable feelings of survivor's guilt.

He had a highly ambivalent relationship with his father; whom he admired and loved on the one hand. On the other hand, he was repeatedly brutally physically beaten by him, which stimulated an intense hatred and resentment in him. In addition, heavy feelings of guilt oppressed him that he—as the youngest son—had left his sick old mother behind in Afghanistan, although it is part of his culture to take care of her:

> I can well understand that these terrible feelings of guilt are so unbearable that sometimes you don't want to live anymore. But I am sure that your mother would rather have a *living* son in Germany than a *dead* one in Afghanistan…

> This interpretation has a great effect. Mr L can successively overcome his state of psychological shock and gradually turn to his own survival in Michaelisdorf. The feelings of guilt continue to be a central theme in the crisis intervention and the long-term psychoanalytic therapy that follows later.

As already described by Radó (1928), the feelings of guilt and the self-destructive punitive impulses could be understood as an attempt to regain the love of the superego (and the internalized father figure). Another line of therapeutic work with this patient was to strengthen the process of disidentification with the (dead) father (see also Taylor, 2010, p. 46).

Thus, in treating chronically depressed patients, understanding the specific inner world of the objects is critical. As Taylor (2007) discusses:

A depressive reaction is more likely when, in the course of development, relationships with inner and outer objects have been established on an insecure and ambivalent footing. Thus, early disappointments with the mother can give rise to a sadistic set of relationships with the mother (the bad mother), and with subsequent mother figures ...

When this potential hatred is eventually turned on the self a depressive state ensures with its characteristic constellations combining resentment, anger and rage leading to persecutory guilt, with identification with the object, attempts to spare it, depressive guilt, reparation, and all the painful emotions of grief. All of these are located in an inner world of thoughts and feelings which fills and preoccupies the patient, and colors all perceptions.

(p. 40/41)

Connected with these processes are pathological idealizations, the hated "bad object" becomes an idealized perfect one. Therefore, it proves to be therapeutically central to distinguish the splits between an idealizing and a persecuting object between the developmentally psychically important transitional phase of an inner distinction between "good" and "bad," which enables the child a first inner orientation.

If the aggressive-destructive impulses as well as splits, idealizations, and devaluations, which were directed against the representation of the lost self or the self, can be revived, recognized, understood, and worked through in the psychoanalytic relationship, this often proves to be decisive for the lasting psychic transformations in the patient. The right timing as well as the right dosage of interpretations of the patient's aggressive-destructive impulses remains an art of the psychoanalytic treatment technique.

It can be difficult for the analyst to deal productively with the intense and relentless destructiveness that sometimes prevails in the inner world of a severely depressed patient and that inevitably manifests itself in the transference-countertransference relationship as well. Since this inner destructiveness is often associated with attacks on psychoanalytic thinking, it can often be experienced as something very concrete in the fantasies of both the patient and the analyst. Fantasies of the most brutal and murderous actions and impulses are often such a vivid fantasy that it is difficult to bear. It may also cause the analyst to fear that interpretations will be experienced by the patient as destructive attacks rather than as empathic aids. Intolerance of such destructive fantasies may tempt the analyst to unconscious enactment, for example, by withdrawing inwardly from the patient or resorting to psychoeducational or other forms of cognitive-behavioral intervention.

Mr M sought psychoanalytic help because he had fallen into a severe depression after his wife's sudden fatal accident. In the first interview, he described a strongly idealized relationship with his wife. At the end of the interview, filled with severe feelings of guilt for having sent his wife on the fatal car trip alone, he suddenly said that he was also "a bad person" because his first idea after hearing the news of his wife's death was: "Now I can finally look for a younger, more attractive wife ...." In the long-term psychoanalytic therapy that followed, it became clear how ambivalent his feelings toward his wife had been. Like his mother (he was an only child), he felt restricted by his wife, controlled, and his personal privacy was hardly respected. Impressively, he soon felt restricted by the analyst and the high-frequency treatment setting as well. "I'm caught here like in a spider's web—and I'm immediately sucked out ...."

Coming to terms with his ambivalent relationships with his close love objects in the outside world, but also in the transference relationship, led to an alleviation of his depressive symptoms and opened up new life perspectives for him in his mature age.

Many psychoanalytic authors describe the importance of reparation and reconciliation as counterbalancing real or fantasized guilt toward the love object for lasting psychological transformations (for more details, see Bleichmar, 1996; Taylor, 2010, 2015).

These processes are crucial when it comes to the question of whether psychoanalysis or psychoanalytic treatment can be completed, a topic we cannot address in detail in this volume. With the group of chronically depressed, early traumatized patients, it has been shown again and again in the empirical psychoanalyses studies how important it is to therapeutically process existing idealizations of the analyst and the associated splitting processes still during the psychoanalytic treatment, so that there is no devaluation of the jointly gained insights and findings after the end of the treatment. Therefore, the critical reflection of what has not been achieved, of disappointments and possibly experienced offenses in the analytic relationship is absolutely crucial for the success of the therapy. The internalization of a "good enough holding and containing, psychoanalytic object" as a counterbalance by the pathological inner objects (especially the sadistically condemning one) described in many variations in the treatment manual and the experience of mature ambivalences is absolutely crucial for the sustainability of the therapeutic results achieved in chronically depressed patients.

It is therefore important in the analytic process to watch out for the danger of "manic reparation," in which the patient in a process of idealizing believes that all problems and conflicts have dissolved, for example, by escaping into mental health. The situation in Germany, that the funding by the Health insurance companies is limited, is particularly suitable for mobilizing such forms of defense in the patient (and sometimes also in the analyst). It is often denied for too long that the funding of psychoanalysis will run out and that it is necessary to think together about whether the treatment can really be completed, whether the patient is able and willing to finance the treatment himself, and so on. This complicates the thorough and demanding working through of the patient's ambivalences in the termination phase of long-term treatments just outlined.

3.3.3 Masochism and the negative therapeutic reaction

Freud already described the phenomenon that in some patients "[...] every partial solution which should result in an improvement or temporary suspension of the symptoms, and in others does, evokes in them a momentary intensification of their suffering; they worsen during the treatment instead of getting better." (Freud, 1923, GW 13, p. 279). He attributed this reaction to unconscious feelings of guilt or an unconscious need for punishment, which psychically forbids the patient any relief, pleasure, or success in treatment.

Kleinian and post-Kleinian authors have discussed that the patient's envy of the analyst's potency and creativity often plays a crucial role. David Taylor (2007) summarizes:

> There appears to be some deep-seated investment, a deep seated masochistic gratification. Which is experienced through defeating the wish, usually located in the object, for life and relief. This is a way of relating to those involved in their care and treatment which, over time, seems designed to create despair and a sense of hopelessness although simultaneously they may be genuinely asking for

help and understanding. Patients in this state seem to be trying to get the therapist/analyst/

G.P., eventually to collude with the despair, and to begin to treat impatiently, harshly, or hurtfully. Both analyst/therapist and patient then go down to failure.

(p. 58/59)

In this context, John Steiner referred to the fable of the scorpion and the frog as illustrations of such self-destructive processes. A scorpion asks a frog to carry him across a river because he cannot swim. The frog agrees because he believes that the scorpion will not sting him during the crossing because otherwise he himself would sink and die. But the scorpion's desire to kill prevails—he stabs the frog in the back and drowns with him.

Thus, some patients find it difficult to endure the painful mourning process that can accompany recovery, in which they have to recognize and acknowledge how much of their lives have been darkened by their depressive illness, how many opportunities they have missed or have been able to use too little for themselves. Some patients also shy away from an improvement of their depressive state because they fear that they might lose the newly gained abilities such as joy, moments of happiness, or trust in close human relationships again: the escape into depression, into the old familiar, seems less dangerous, safer and less painful to them: in this way, they virtually anticipate the feared disappointment, actively manufacture the relapse so as not to be passively surprised by it.

Another source of relapse after improvement of depression may be related to an unconscious conflict of autonomy and separation toward the end of the treatment, a prohibition to enjoy the fruits of the joint work and to continue autonomously his recovery process without the analyst. In some supervisions of the LAC study, it could be recognized that the analyst—also unconsciously—stimulated such conflicts insofar as he in turn denied or did not adequately process the pending separation from the analysand, to put it drastically, could not release the analysand from therapeutic dependence.

3.3.4 *Ego ideal and superego*

Both David Taylor and Hugo Bleichmar discuss in detail the specific treatment problems in dealing with pathological ego ideal and superego structures in psychoanalysis with chronically depressed patients.

> These masochistic and sadistic internal relationships are mediated through super-ego structures which attempt to protect, or to accuse, the self and/or the object on the basis of good and bad qualities and impulses, or right (justified) or wrong (unjustified) motives. In depression and melancholia, these moral judgments cease to be helpful [...]
>
> In more ill patients the super-ego structure is highly abnormal and primitive (v.i.). It is full of destructive and aggressive impulses which may dismantle or denude important ego functions, or be highly dangerous to the self (suicide) or sometimes, more rarely, to others.
>
> (Taylor, 2007, p. 41)

For all the psychoanalytic study therapists in the LAC study, these concepts were very relevant in the treatment of chronically depressed patients. In the clinical conferences, it was repeatedly noticed how broad the spectrum in treatment techniques was among the study therapists in order to avoid unconscious entanglement of their own ego-ideal and superego conflicts with those of the patient. Some analysts developed a fine sense of humor to caricature the rigidity of ego-ideal and superego of an analytic treatment and thereby make it accessible to critical reflection in the analytic treatment. Often the analysands then identified with this psychoanalytic attitude.

The extensive case example of the psychoanalysis with Mr A, which is presented in Chapter 4, can illustrate this. Mr A himself demanded a high-frequency treatment because he thought that the analyst "would not reach him emotionally with just one session a week." He had an inkling that in a low-frequency treatment setting his rigid superego and ego ideal could hardly be modified therapeutically. In the early stages of psychoanalysis he suffered from terrible nightmares of falling into deep chasms, being locked in tunnels, being flooded by the sea, etc. We understood these themes in the context of his severe traumatizations due to growing up with a depressed, alcoholic primary object. In the short summary of the psychoanalyses it is discussed that the nightmares decreased in the course of treatment. The dreams changed systematically: the dreamer regained his self-agency, was not alone anymore but often in company with helping objects, and even showed humor and successful problem-solving in his dreams (see Chapter 4).

3.3.5 Narcissistic vulnerability, self-regulation, and identity conflicts

Dealing with the extreme narcissistic vulnerability of chronically depressed, early traumatized patients must be constantly considered in treatments. "The depressive state thus consists not only of the un-realizability of the wish but also, and more significantly, of a *self-representation as powerless to fulfil the wish, to impose upon one's life.*" (Bleichmar, 1996, p. 936). Bibring (1952) already pointed out that this experience of powerlessness is central to depression. People who have experienced massive powerlessness and helplessness in their childhood are particularly prone to develop severe depression later on.

In some cases, narcissistic personality disorder may even be considered the primary cause of chronic depression (see the pathway at the top of Bleichmar's chart, right side, Figure 3.1).

> Certain narcissistic personalities (those who fit Kernberg's description of this disorder and who display grandiose fantasies, omnipotence, denigration of the object, destructive aggression, etc.) (Kernberg, 1976) get depressed when they cannot satisfy their grandiose fantasies. Depression sets in when they have to bear what they perceive as the humiliation of not being able to give their aggression free reign, which makes them feel they do not attain the desired identification with an omnipotent, destructive, ideal self (Kernberg, 1976).
>
> (Bleichmar, 1996, p. 938)

The therapeutic treatment of narcissistic vulnerability in certain groups of patients by specific psychoanalytic techniques (supportive versus interpretive, etc.) has been widely discussed in the psychoanalytic literature. Thus, some manuals of brief psychoanalytic therapy emphasize the need to establish a supportive working alliance characterized by trust and security in the initial phase of treatment.

We have discussed above (cf. 3.2) that the breakdown of primal trust ("Urvertrauen") is one of the main characteristics of traumatized patients. Therefore, we think here of other treatment techniques that also aim to regain a spark of hope for a trusting (therapeutic) relationship, especially in these patients, but use a psychoanalytic treatment technique that is different from psychoeducational or supportive techniques (such as giving advice, responding with positive feedback to so behavior of the patient, etc.). In many psychoanalyses in our studies it was impressively shown that in the patient such a glimmer of hope in an alternative, reliable therapeutic relationship could be developed in the initial phase of treatment precisely by a genuinely psychoanalytic attitude of the study therapist. The continuous professional attention of the analyst, his holding and containing functions in a reliable, predictable treatment setting were crucial for understanding the collapsed trust in a helping object and its consequences. Psychoanalytically, embodied memories of positive early relational experiences with the primary object are presumably psychically revived through such a reliable, positively affectively toned, "neutral" professional relationship. In pathological object relationships, too, there were usually islands of such supporting positive relational experiences on which the analytic relationship can build on (see Chapter 4).

Together with the professional, empathic object, the analysand was successively more able to bear in mind the consequences of the experienced traumatizations for the inner object world and thus to relativize their influence to some extent. This process of understanding, fostered by the analyst's constant, reliable, and emphatic attention, strengthened the patient's narcissistic self-esteem regulation, so that in later phases of psychoanalysis he could bear to perceive, for example, his own aggressive-destructive fantasies and impulses without exposing himself too much to the sadistic-destructive condemnations by his rigid superego. It is important to emphasize that these processes were fostered by a characteristic professional attitude of the analyst, as is characteristic of psychoanalysis.

In a detailed case study of Mrs B we tried to illustrate this (see Leuzinger-Bohleber et al., 2019). The severely traumatized 24-year-old young woman had to control the psychoanalytic situation almost completely for many months. Her aggressive-destructive impulses, which were massively perceptible in the analyst's countertransference, could not be directly addressed

for a long time because the analyst felt that Mrs B would experience such an interpretation as an attack on her already very
unstable self.

The psychoanalyst therefore tried to endure the situation
emotionally somehow and to maintain her psychoanalytic interest in the patient and her curiosity for her intolerable behavior
in the analytic sessions. Mrs. B., in her third year of analysis,
told us that she had been very aware of this attitude on the part
of the analyst.—"I kept waiting for you to get impatient and
lecture me or even send me away, as the CBT therapist did ...."

It was only at this point that the analysand realized how
much she had needed the psychoanalytic sessions and the analyst's cautious approach during the first two years of treatment
to regain her narcissistic self-regulation, which had collapsed
due to the traumatic loss of her father after his heart attack as an
eight-year-old girl and her growing up with a psychotic mother.
In parallel, she regained a spark of epistemic trust in a helping
object. Only then could she dispense with the constant talking
in the analytic sessions and engage in a thoughtful psychoanalytic process with interpretations in the narrower sense at all.

3.3.6   Deficit of ego resources, mania,
and psychotic depression

We excluded psychotic patients in both the LAC and MODE studies.
Nevertheless, in individual cases, patients diagnosed as depressed at
the beginning of treatment in the diagnostical interview regressed to
a psychotic level of mental functioning during the psychoanalyses. As
Bleichmar (1996) points out, in these cases in addition to biographical experience, certain unexpected life circumstances had led to ego
deficits:

Any condition, that produces ego deficits (inner conflicts, traumatic
reality, parents' ego deficits, etc.), diminishes the possibilities for
sublimation, for establishing satisfactory relationships, for being
able to take advantage of real-life opportunities, for compensat-
ing losses. The subject thus comes to feel helpless and powerless
to fulfill his/her wishes. In some cases of pathological mourning

following the loss of a job or of a loved one (death, divorce, etc.), the subject's incapacity to get a new object because of his/her lack of ego resources, determines that the lost object begins to undergo a progressive process of idealization.

(p. 946/947)

In a LIFE interview after a year of low-frequency psychoanalysis in the frame of the MODE study, the blinded psychologist noted that the patient had developed some severe psychotic symptoms. It turned out that she had developed a severe negative therapeutic reaction in her psychoanalysis. In consultation with the analyst, the clinical principal investigator of MODE offered the patient several interviews so that a change of analyst could finally be made. In this way, it was possible to help the patient out of the psychotic regression, overcome the severe crisis, and finally continue her psychoanalytic process although with a new psychoanalyst.

This is an example that may illustrate that sometimes the research setting was able to assume an important triangulation function in a few problematic single cases.

At the same time, this case example also might illustrate that transference phenomena must be carefully reflected on both the project leaders and the psychological team.

3.3.7 Transgenerational aspects

This basic feeling of being embedded in a meaning-bearing way in the generational sequence is a point of view that hardly appears in the scientific discussion of transgenerational aspects of depression and trauma, although there is now a broad field of research dealing with this topic. We cannot discuss in this framework the fascinating attempts to integrate genetic/epigenetic, psychological, and sociological research findings on the transgenerational transmission of trauma, but must refer to them here (recent review, e.g., in Böker, 2011; Jiménez, Botto & Fonagy, 2021).

As mentioned in Section 3.2: psychoanalytic knowledge about the short- and long-term effects of severe traumatization comes mainly from clinical work with survivors of the Shoah and their children and grandchildren. The secret of the severely traumatized parents can settle like a "phantom" in the children's unconscious and determine their actions, thoughts, and feelings without being recognized (Abraham, cited in Bohleber, 2010). The trauma of the parents becomes an "organizing factor" in the lives of the children (Bergmann & Jucovy, 1982, p. 51). Kestenberg (1980) speaks of a "survival complex" that is passed on to children as common ground. Unconsciously, the child is expected to undo the affectively charged traumas that destroyed the psychological structure of the parents. For the child, this means that his or her person represents a psychic space for desires, fears, and affects that are not his or her own but have been inscribed upon him or her. Because of the close connection to the parents, it is not possible for the child to recognize them as strangers and to assert his autonomy. In psychoanalytic literature, two main fantasies are described. (1) The child acts as a substitute for a murdered beloved family member. (2) The child is seen as having a special mission: to restore family pride and heal past injuries through personal achievements and life goals.

> By adopting these parental fantasies, the child takes shelter of the traumatized adults and justifies their often cruel or abstruse behavior. It tries to help them and thus maintains the close relationship with them. The parent-child relationship has a strong symbiotic character. The process of individuation and separation of children poses a serious threat to the family equilibrium, because the separation of the child could reawaken old fears of annihilation in the parents ....
>
> (Bohleber, 2010, p. 107, translation M.LB)

Faimberg (1987) therefore speaks of the "telescoping" of generations. The boundaries between generations are pushed together: one's own life is unconsciously merged with that of one's parents (see also Section 3.2). Yolanda Gampel (1982) uses the powerful metaphor of a "fallout." In doing so, she invokes the horrors of the destruction of Hiroshima and Nagasaki by the atomic bombs dropped by the United States in their impact. With her metaphor of the "fallout" Gampel describes the all-pervasive effects of massive psychological trauma left in the atmosphere of the family of Shoah survivors. Ilany Kogan (1995), like other authors, uses the metaphor of the black hole. Extreme traumatization acts unrecognized as a devouring center of energy that determines not only the psychological experiences of the first generation of Holocaust survivors but also the second. As a result, children constantly live in two realities, their parents' past on the one hand and their own present on the other. Often, a disturbed experience of time, partial identity diffusion, and a sense of fragmented identity are among the consequences of such unrecognized identifications. This is one of the reasons why in Hans Keilson's (1979) study it was so crucial for the long-term consequences of Shoah orphans—in the third phase of traumatization—whether the children's Jewish identity was recognized, supported, and publicly addressed.

As already mentioned in Section 3.2, in many psychoanalyses of the LAC study, *the transgenerational dimension of depressive illness* became very clear. The psychoanalysis of Mr A which is summarized quite extensively in the following Chapter 4 may illustrate this finding. Another, shorter case illustration of this topic will be presented in Section 5.3.

Notes

1 This chapter is a modified and enlarged translation of the chapter 3 in Leuzinger-Bohleber, Fischmann & Beutel (2022) written by M. Leuzinger-Bohleber.

2 David Taylor (2015) draws predominantly on the Kleinian tradition just outlined in his treatment manual for depression. *"The goals and values incorporated in the manual are based on the central contributions of Freud, Klein, and Bion, as well as suggestions from literary works by, for example, W. H. Auden (1940), Thomas Mann (1956), psychoanalysts such as Roger Money-Kyrle (1956), and philosophers such as Paul Ricouer (1977) and Richard Wollheim"* (p. 7).

3 Surprisingly Joel Whitebook (2017/2018) places the topic of "depression and trauma" at the center of his new, "Intellectual biography" of Sigmund Freud. He describes that Freud himself had experienced serious early traumas through several losses and growing up with a depressive mother, which—hardly critically reflected by himself—shaped his personality, his theorizations and even his understanding of science: *"The boundless anxiety that was very likely to overtake him repeatedly in his first three and a half years, and his inability to alleviate it by his own efforts, sowed in him the seeds of a lifelong hatred of passivity, helplessness, and dependence ...so we are not surprised to find helplessness as a central aspect of his theory of human nature."* (Whitebook, 2018, p. 62). *"Freud's Doctrine of Helplessness (German in original) is a biologically based elaboration of the philosophical theme of the finitude of man. It makes it possible to draw a direct line from Kant, the Enlightenment philosopher (German in original) to Freud, the representative of the dark Enlightenment. Like Kant,*

> *Freud saw the goal of the Enlightenment in overcoming immaturity. But while Kant conceives this immaturity primarily philosophically, Freud explains it quite concretely anthropologically" (p. 390,* translation M.LB).

The biographical underpinnings of Whitebook's thesis may be controversial. What is undisputed, however, is that Freud placed the effects of helplessness, powerlessness, and extreme stimulus overload of the ego at the center of his conceptualizations of trauma in his analysis of "war neuroses" after World War I (see Makari, 2008, among others).

4 Joint work by Leuzinger-Bohleber and Rolf Pfeifer played a major role for a new clinical understanding of embodied memories particularly in psychoanalyses with severely early traumatized patients (see, among others, Leuzinger-Bohleber & Pfeifer, 2002); on the problems in the philosophy and theory of science associated with this dialogue, see, among others, Hampe, 2003; Leuzinger-Bohleber, Emde & Pfeifer, 2013; Gallese, 2013a, 2013b). These papers tried to throw a new perspective on well-known concepts, such as "scenic understanding" (Argelander, 1970 [im LV sind zwei Quellen von 1970—welche ist die richtige?]; Lorenzer, 1974), but also "listening with the third ear" (Reik, 1948), "cracking-up" (Bollas, 1995), or the "now moments" of the Boston Change Process Study Group.

5 Alfred Lorenzer, then a scientist at the Sigmund Freud Institute, was one of the first pioneers to recognize the relevance of the dialogue with neuroscience for psychoanalysis as early as the 1970s. Lorenzer (2002) already postulated at that time that interaction experiences during the embryonic period and the first months of life are "embodied," that is, imprinted in sensorimotor reaction patterns of the body and—unconsciously—determine later information processing processes in an adequate or inadequate ("neurotic") manner—an insight which is now also confirmed by empirical researchers investigating the importance of resonant, interactive processes for the early development of the self as well as the effects of early traumatization, but conceptualized in a different way.

6 The following section is a modification and translation of Chapter 5 in Leuzinger-Bohleber, Fischmann and Beutel (2022). I was the main author of this chapter.

7 We follow the graph of Bleichmar (see Figure 3.1).

8 The STEP-BY-STEP project was a pilot project initiated by the Hessian Ministry in 2015 for the care of traumatized refugees in the initial reception facility "Michaelisdorf" in Darmstadt realized under the leadership of M. Leuzinger-Bohleber and S. Andresen until 2017 (cf. Leuzinger-Bohleber et al., 2016).

References

Abraham, K. (1911). *Giovanni Segantini. A Psychoanalytic Experiment. Schriften Zur Angewandten Seelenkunde.* Vol. 11. Leipzig: Deuticke.

Abraham, K. (1924). *Attempt at a History of the Development of the Libido Based on the Psychoanalysis of Mental Disorders.* Leipzig: Internationaler Psychoanalytischer Verlag.

Abraham, N., & Torok, M. (1994). *The Shell and the Kernel: Renewals of Psychoanalysis*. Vol. 1. Chicago: University of Chicago Press.

Argelander, H. (1970). Die szenische funktion des ichs und ihr anteil an der symptom- und charakterbildung. *Psyche—Z Psychoanal*, *24*(5), 325–345.

Auerhahn, N. C., & Laub, D. (1998). Intergenerational memory of the Holocaust. In Y. Danieli (Ed.), *International Handbook of Multigenerational Legacies of Trauma* (pp. 21–41). New York: Plenum Press. https://doi.org/10.1007/978-1-4757-5567-1_2

Bergmann, M. S., & Jucovy, M. E. (1982). *Generations of the Holocaust*. New York: Columbia University Press.

Bibring, E. (1952). Das problem der depression. *Psyche—Z Psychoanal*, *6*, 81–101.

Blatt, S. J. (2004). *Experiences of depression: Theoretical, Clinical, and Research Perspectives*. New York: American Psychological Association.

Blatt, S. J., & Zuroff, D. C. (2005). Empirical evaluation of the assumptions in identifying evidence-based treatments in mental health. *Clinical Psychology Review*, *25*(4), 459–486.

Bleichmar, H. (2010). Rethinking pathological mourning: Multiple types and therapeutic approaches. *The Psychoanalytic Quarterly*, *79*(1), 71–93.

Bleichmar, H. B. (1996). Some subtypes of depression and their implications for psychoanalytic treatment. *International Journal of Psychoanalysis*, *77*(5), 935–961.

Bohleber, W. (2005). Zur psychoanalyse der depression. Erscheinungsformen—behandlung—erklärungsansätze. *Psyche—Z Psychoanal*, *59*(9–10), 781–788. https://doi.org/10.21706/ps-59-9-781

Bohleber, W. (2010). *Was Psychoanalyse heute leistet. Identität und Intersubjektivität, Trauma und Therapie, Gewalt und Gesellschaft*. Stuttgart: Klett-Cotta. In English (not identical publication): Bohleber, W. (2012). *Destructiveness, Intersubjectivity, and Trauma: The Identity Crisis of Modern Psychoanalysis*. London: Karnac.

Bohleber, W., & Leuzinger-Bohleber, M. (2016). The special problem of interpretation in the treatment of traumatized patients. *Psychoanalytic Inquiry*, *36*(1), 60–76.

Böker, H. (2011). *Psychotherapy of Depression*. Bern: Huber.

Bollas, C. (1995). *Cracking-up: Work of Unconscious Experience*. London: Routledge.

Cooper, A. M. (1986). Toward a limited definition of psychic trauma. In A. Rothstein (Ed.), *The Reconstruction of Trauma: Its Significance in Clinical Work* (pp. 41–56). Madison, Connecticut: International Universities Press, Inc.

Cournut, J. (1988). A residue that connects. The unconscious sense of guilt concerning the borrowed. *Yearbook of Psychoanalysis*, *22*(1), 67–98.

Damasio, A. R. (1994). *Descartes Errors. Emotion, Reason, and the Human Brain*. New York, NY: Penguin Group.

Edelman, G. M. (1987). *Neural Darwinism. The Theory of Neuronal Group Selection*. New York, NY: Basic Books.

Edelman, G. M. (1989). *The Remembered Present: A Biological Theory of Consciousness*. New York, NY: Basic Books.

Faimberg, H. (1987). The telescoping of generations. On the genealogy of certain identifications. *Yearbook of Psychoanalysis, 20*(S), 114–142.

Freud, S. (1916/1917). *Mourning and Melancholy* (Collected works). Vol. XII, p. 428. Frankfurt a.m.: Fischer.

Freud, S. (1923/2000). *The Ego and the Id. Sigmund Freud Studienausgabe, 3*, 273–330.

Gabbard, G. (2018). *How Psychoanalysis Changes Us: The Effect of Psychoanalysis on Both Patient and Analyst*. Unpublished introductory paper given at the Symposium 2018: On change. New York: Mount Sinai Medical Center, April 14, 2018.

Gaensbauer, T. J. (1995). Trauma in the preverbal period: Symptoms, memories, and developmental impact. *The Psychoanalytic Study of the Child, 50*(1), 122–149.

Gaensbauer, T. J. (2011). Embodied simulation, mirror neurons, and the reenactment of trauma in early childhood. *Neuropsychoanalysis, 13*, 91–107.

Gallese, V. (2013a). Mirror neurons, embodied simulation and a second-person approach to mind-reading. *Cortex, 49*, 2954–2956.

Gallese, V. (2013b). Finding the body in the brain. Conceptual reflections on mirror neurons. In M. Leuzinger-Bohleber, R. N. Emde & R. Pfeifer (Eds.), *Embodiment: An Innovative Concept for Developmental Research and Psychoanalysis* (pp. 75–112). CT: Göttingen and Bristol.

Gampel, Y. (1982). A daughter of silence. In M. S. Bergman & M. E. Jucovy (Eds.), *Generations of the Holocaust* (pp. 120–136). New York: Basic.

Green, A. (2007). Pulsions de destruction et maladies somatiques. *Revue Française De Psychosomatique, 2*, 45–70.

Grubrich-Simitis, I. (1979). Extreme traumatization as cumulative trauma: Psychoanalytic studies of mental after-effects of concentration camp imprisonment. *Psyche—Z Psychoanal, 33*(11), 991–1023.

Hagmann, G. (1995). Mourning: A review and reconsideration. *International Journal of Psychoanalysis, 76*, 909–925.

Hampe, M. (2003). Plurality of science and the unity of reason. In M. Leuzinger-Bohleber, A. U. Dreher & J. Canestri (Eds.), *Pluralism and Unity? Methods of Research in Psychoanalysis* (pp. 45–63). (The International Psychoanalysis Library) London: International Psychoanalytical Association.

Hauser, S. T. (2008). The interplay of genes, environments, and psychoanalysis. *Journal of the American Psychoanalytic Association, 56*, 509–514.

Jacobson, E. (1971). On the psychoanalytic theory of affects. *Depression: Comparative Studies of Normal, Neurotic, and Psychotic Conditions*. New York: International Universities Press.

Jiménez, J. P., Botto, A., & Fonagy, P. (Eds.) (2021). *Etiopathogenic Theories and Models in Depression*. Cham, Switzerland: Springer. https://doi.org/10.1007/978-3-030-77329-8

Joffe, W. G., & Sandler, J. (1965). Notes on pain, depression, and individuation. *The Psychoanalytic Study of the Child, 20*(1), 394–424.

Keilson, H. (1979). *Sequential Traumatization in Children: Descriptive-Clinical & Quantifying-Statistical Follow-up Study on the Fate of Jewish War Orphans in d. Netherlands*: Enke.

Keilson, H., Sarphatie, H. R., Bearne, Y. T., Coleman, H. T., & Winter, D. T. (1992). *Sequential Traumatization in Children: A Clinical and Statistical Follow-Up Study on the Fate of the Jewish War Orphans in the Netherlands*. Jerusalem: Magnes Press.

Kernberg, O. F. (2009). An integrated theory of depression. *Neuropsychoanalysis, 11*(1), 76–80.

Kernberg, O. F. (1976). Technical considerations in the treatment of borderline personality organization. *Journal of the American Psychoanalytic Association, 24*(4), 795–829.

Kestenberg, J. S. (1980). Psychoanalyses of children of survivors from the Holocaust: Case presentations and assessment. *Journal of the American Psychoanalytic Association, 28*(4), 775–804.

Khan, M. (1964). Ego distortion, cumulative trauma, and the role of reconstruction in the analytic situation. *International Journal of Psychoanalysis, 45*, 272–279.

Kind, J. S. (1992). *Die Psychoökonomie einer Suche*. Göttingen: Vandenhoeck.

Kogan, I. (1995). *The Cry of Mute Children: A Psychoanalytic Perspective of the Second Generation of the Holocaust*. London: Free Assn Books.

Krystal, H. (1988). *Integration and Self-Healing. Affect, Trauma, Alexithymia*. Hillsdale, NJ: The Analytic Press.

Lakoff, G., & Johnson, M. (1999). *Philosophy in the Flesh: The Embodied Mind and Its Challenge to Western Thought*. New York: Basic Books.

Laub, D. (2005). From speechlessness to narrative: The cases of Holocaust historians and of psychiatrically hospitalized survivors. *Literature and Medicine, 24*(2), 253–265.

Leuzinger-Bohleber, M. (2003). The long shadows of war and persecution: War children in psychoanalyses. Observations and reports from the DPV Catamnesis study. *Psyche—Z Psychoanal, 57*, 982–1016.

Leuzinger-Bohleber, M.; Stuhr, U.; Rüger, B.; Beutel, M. (2003). How to study the 'quality of psychoanalytic treatments' and their long-term effects on patient's well-being. A representative, multi-perspective follow-up study. *The International Journal of Psychoanalysis, 84*, 263–290.

Leuzinger-Bohleber, M. (2015a). *Finding the Body in the Mind—Embodied Memories, Trauma, and Depression*. London: Karnac: International Psychoanalytical Association.

Leuzinger-Bohleber, M. (2021). Contemporary psychodynamic theories on depression. In J. P. Jiménez, A. Botto & P. Fonagy (Eds.), *Etiopathogenic Theories and Models in Depression* (pp. 91–112). Cham, Switzerland: Springer.

Leuzinger-Bohleber, M., & Pfeifer, R. (2002). Remembering a depressive primary object? Memory in the dialogue between psychoanalysis and cognitive science. *International Journal of Psychoanalysis, 83*, 3–33.

Leuzinger-Bohleber, M., Emde, R. N., & Pfeifer, R. (2013). *Embodiment: An Innovative Concept for Developmental Research and Psychoanalysis*. Göttingen: Vandenhoeck & Ruprecht.

Leuzinger-Bohleber, M., Fischmann, T., & Beutel, M. E. (2022). *Chronische Depression. Psychoanalytische Langzeittherapie*. Reihe: Praxis der psychodynamischen Psychotherapie—analytische und tiefenpsychologisch fundierte Psychotherapie, Bd. 12. Göttingen: Hogrefe Verlag.

Leuzinger-Bohleber, M., Rickmeyer, C., Tahiri, M., & Hettich, N. (2016). Special communication. What can psychoanalysis contribute to the current refugee crisis? Preliminary reports from STEP-BY-STEP: A psychoanalytic pilot project for supporting refugees in a "first reception camp" and crisis interventions with traumatized refugees. *International Journal of Psychoanalysis, 97*(4), 1077–1093. https://doi.org/10.1111/1745-8315.12542

Leuzinger-Bohleber, M., Kaufhold, J., Kallenbach, L., Negele, A., Ernst, M., Keller, W., & Beutel, M. (2019). How to measure sustained psychic transformations in long-term treatments of chronically depressed patients: Symptomatic and structural changes in the LAC depression study of the outcome of cognitive-behavioural and psychoanalytic long-term treatments. *International Journal of Psychoanalysis, 100*(1), 99–127.

Levine, H. B., Reed, G. S., & Scarfone, D. (2013). *Unrepresented States and the Construction of Meaning: Clinical and Theoretical Contributions*. London: Karnac.

Loch, W., & Kutter, P. (1967). *The Theory of Illness in Psychoanalysis*. W. Loch (Ed.). Stuttgart: Hirzel.

Lorenzer, A. (1974). *The Truth of Psychoanalytic Cognition. A Historical-Materialist Sketch*. Frankfurt am Main: Suhrkamp.

Lorenzer, A. (2002). *Language, Meaning, and the Unconscious: Basic Psychoanalytic Understanding and Neuroscience*. Stuttgart: Klett-Cotta.

Makari, G. (2008). *Revolution in Mind: The Creation of Psychoanalysis*. Melbourne: Univ. Publishing.

Mentzos, S. (1995). *Depression and Mania. Psychodynamics and Therapy of Affective Disorders*. Göttingen: Vandenhoeck & Ruprecht.

Mizen, R. (2009). The embodied mind. *Journal of Analytical Psychology, 54*(2), 253–272. https://doi.org/10.1111/j.1468-5922.2009.01773.x

Pfeifer, R., & Bongard, J. (2007). *How the Body Shapes the Way We Think: A New View of Intelligence*. Cambridge, MA: The MIT Press.

Radebold, H., Heuft, G., & Fooken, I. (Eds.) (2006). *Kindheiten im Zweiten Weltkrieg: Kriegserfahrungen und deren Folgen aus psychohistorischer Perspektive*. Weinheim, München: Beltz Juventa.

Radó, S. (1928). The problem of melancholia. *International Journal of Psychoanalysis, 9*, 420–438.

Reed, G. (2013). An empty mirror: Reflections on nonrepresentation. In H. B. Levine, G. S. Reed & D. Scarfone (Eds.), *Unrepresented States and the Construction of Meaning: Clinical and Theoretical Contributions* (pp. 18–41). London: Karnac.

Reik, T. (1948). *Listening With the Third Ear: The Inner Experience of a Psychoanalyst*. New York: Farrar, Straus & Co.

Ringel, E., & Sonneck, G. (1978). Presuicidal syndrome and social structure. In H. Pohlmeier (Ed.), *Suicide Prevention, Presumption or Obligation* (pp. 105–121). Bonn: Keil Verlag.

Scarfone, D. (2013). A brief introduction to the work of Jean Laplanche. *International Journal of Psychoanalysis, 94*, 545–566.

Taylor, D. (2007). Treatment Manual for Tavistock Adult Depression Study. Unpublished manuscript.

Taylor, D. (2010). Tavistock Manual of psychoanalytic psychotherapy. *Psyche—Z Psychoanal, 64*, 833–886.

Taylor, D. (2015). Treatment manuals and the advancement of psychoanalytic knowledge: The treatment manual of the Tavistock adult depression study. *International Journal of Psychoanalysis, 96*(3), 845–875.

Whitebook, J. (2017/2018). *Freud. An Intellectual Biography*. New York: Cambridge University Press. (Deutsch, Stuttgart: Klett Cotta).

Will, H. (1994). Phenomenology of depression from the psychoanalytic viewpoint. *Psyche—Z Psychoanal, 48*(4), 361–385.

Will, H., Grabenstedt, Y., Banck, G., & Volkl, G. (2008). *Depression: Psychodynamik Und Therapie*. Stuttgart: W. Kohlhammer Verlag.

Chapter 4

"As far back as I can remember, I was always depressed …" From a psychoanalysis with a chronic depressed, traumatized patient[1]

4.1 Preliminary remarks

The following relatively detailed summary of psychoanalysis combines previous conceptual, clinical, and empirically based psychoanalytic insights into the psychodynamics of depression with some concrete impressions from psychoanalytic clinical practice. This reveals the multi-layered and complex nature of the psychodynamics of chronic depression and its close interweaving with traumatic experiences

Of course, this summary can only describe a few highlights from the several hundred analytic sessions. In order to select these somewhat less randomly, the focus is placed on analytical sessions in which important dreams were recounted, because dreams are still regarded as the via regia to the unconscious in today's psychoanalysis. Therefore, the manifest dream contents and structures as well as the psychoanalytic understanding of the latent meaning of the dream in the transference are indicators of psychic transformations that the analysand undergoes in his inner world in the course of psychoanalysis (see e.g. Leuzinger-Bohleber et al., in press).

In other publications, we have discussed in detail the opportunities, but also the pitfalls of narrative summaries of psychoanalyses (cf. Leuzinger-Bohleber, Grabhorn & Bahrke, 2020). In order to critically and transparently counter some of the dangers, such as the random selection of clinical material, the neglect of problematic observations in the sense of a wish-fulfilling view of the author, etc., in the context of a scientific study, this psychoanalysis was discussed in detail in a group of experts with the help of the so-called *Three-Level-Model of Clinical Observation.*[2] As discussed in detail, this method can be used to jointly approach the "narrative truth" of complex psychoanalytic

DOI: 10.4324/9781003455349-4

observations in psychoanalysis (cf. De Leon de Bernardi & Leuzinger-Bohleber, 2021).

4.2 Assessment interviews

Although this was a few years ago, my first impression of Mr A is still very clear to me: he is in his mid-forties, a slender, fragile-looking man who doesn't dare to look at me. His almost anorexic physique reminds me of the figures of the Swiss painter Alberto Giacometti.

He speaks in a low, barely understandable voice and reports that he has actually always been depressed, but that this condition has continued to worsen over the last two years. He was no longer able to concentrate at work and could hardly eat or sleep, partly because of the terrible nightmares … He has therefore been on sick leave for eight weeks now and spends his days alone in bed in a darkened room. "I don't see any point in anything anymore, I just want to get everything over with …. " In the end, his wife was so desperate that she cried and asked him to get help.

When I ask him if anything has triggered this condition, he remains silent for a long time. "I haven't made a connection yet, but my wife was 8 weeks pregnant, but lost the child six months ago—I was very sad, I was really looking forward to the child—and this is probably the end. It is the 3rd miscarriage and my wife is now already 42 …."—"It may well be that this disappointment has plunged you into this deep feeling of futility. Perhaps you unconsciously didn't want to make a connection between your crisis and the miscarriage, also to protect your wife from your reproaches …." —After a long pause Mr A comments: "That may be true, my wife has been very sad herself, I didn't want to burden her with my grief … ."

After another long pause, I finally dare to ask him to tell me a bit more about his situation and his life story … It turns out that he is a scientist and works for a large company. He met his wife during his studies—she was his first love when he was 32 years old and his great happiness. He feels less lonely now that he is married. "We both wanted children so much, but perhaps we waited too long—it's more difficult to get pregnant in your late 30s …." After another long pause, he says thoughtfully: "Maybe I also hesitated so long to become a father because I experienced a lot of misery in my family. I have no memories of the first years of my life, but I do remember elementary school, when my mother slipped into alcoholism. It was terrible. We had to hide alcoholic drinks from her or even take them away from her. She was angry, nasty, uncontrollable, shouted at us or was simply drunk. My father was very helpless and took refuge in work. He left everything to me and my brother—alcoholism overshadowed my entire childhood and youth … ." It becomes clear to me what a lonely, socially isolated and overwhelmed child Mr A probably has been. Growing up with a traumatized mother must have had a major impact on him.

During the assessment interviews, I was impressed by the patient's self-reflective abilities. For example, he reported that he kept dreaming of *standing on a high object, e.g. a bookshelf, which suddenly began to sway beneath him. It sways more and more until he finally falls off and wakes up in a panic*. He himself makes a connection to his mother's alcohol addiction, which led to the floor literally "swaying beneath his feet" during his primary school years. The addiction plunged the whole family into the abyss.

The patient responds to the attempt to understand this dream together with another dream, which he tells me in the second interview and which, in my opinion, also speaks to the hope he has for psychoanalysis: "I'm on my bike, wanting to reach some destination … then suddenly I'm standing in front of an abyss. I see my brother and a friend down in the valley. I take a large ladder and want to climb down to them into the abyss. But as I'm standing on the ladder, it starts to wobble—it wobbles and wobbles, so I'm afraid of falling off. My brother's companion calls out to me that it won't work and that I should climbing back up the ladder and take the path further down to the right … I follow his advice and actually find the way down …." The patient tells me that this is the first dream in which he is not alone and from which he does not wake up in a panic, but finds a solution based on the advice of another person. In this we see his hope of finding a way out of his loneliness with the help of psychoanalysis and of leaving the "wobbly ladder" behind him, prognostically an indicator of the beginning of a positive transference.

His nightmares touch me very much, also because I suspect that they contain unconscious memories of early traumatization, so-called embodied memories. This is why Mr A seems very fragile to me. I suggest that he start with a one-session sitting psychoanalytic therapy. To my astonishment, Mr A responds: "Mrs Bohleber, I don't think that's a good idea. One session a week is not enough for me. I'll have forgotten everything by a week from now. I don't think you can reach me emotionally with one hour a week—that's not enough …"—I take Mr A's view very seriously and offer him a three-session psychoanalysis, even though I don't actually have any free analysis slots.—The following summary of the course of the analysis illustrates that Mr A was right in his intuitive view: he really did need psychoanalysis!

4.3   Highlights of a psychoanalysis[3]

4.3.1   Nightmares—and early enactments of trauma in the transference

Mr A appears to be highly motivated for treatment and hardly ever cancels an analytical session. In the first few months of treatment, the conflicts at work escalate. He often feels unable to concentrate or work creatively.

Many analytical sessions are about depressive self-reproach, massive feelings of inferiority and the unconscious conviction of being "a strange loner that nobody likes, let alone loves …." It is often difficult to reach the analysand emotionally—he seems tense on the couch, usually speaks very quietly, often barely understandable to me and seems to be preparing for the sessions. It is noticeable that he is afraid of not being able to please me either, of being "a strange bird" (ein "komischer Vogel") who bores me.

It is, therefore, a gift for both of us that Mr A often remembers dreams. They seem to be like something "third" that we turn to together without getting too close to each other personally. The closeness and dependence on me seem to cause Mr A great anxiety.

As I have already mentioned, Mr A suffers from prolific nightmares. So it obviously relieves him that he can tell them to me in the sessions and thus remains less alone with them. The content of the dreams is usually terrible: the dreamer is flooded by storm waves, stuck in narrow canals, tormented or persecuted. After a conflict at work, for example, he dreamt: *I was sentenced to death and wanted to hang myself on death row … I woke up in a panic …* Dreams like this (and many others in this period of psychoanalysis) can illustrate the enormous feelings of helplessness and archaic forms of guilt. These feelings seem to be at the heart of Mr A's depression: a basic sense of being a passive victim of strokes of fate against which he can do nothing, absolutely nothing. This was probably a dominant feeling in his everyday life during the first 12 years of his life, when he often did not know whether he would find his mother alive after school or whether she had fallen down the cellar stairs drunk and died. Emotionally almost unbearable memories come to his mind: once the two brothers found their mother naked on the toilet in excrement and vomit—it was not clear whether she was without consciousness or simply totally drunk. The father was not present in this scene either—he seems to have taken refuge in his job and left the domestic misery to his two children.

In this way, in the analytic situation and also in the transference relationship with me, something of the traumatogenic object relationship with his mother is re-enacted. Thus, the analytic relationship in these first weeks still seems very fragile. Mr A also seems to struggle with my unconscious conviction that he cannot rely on his close attachment figures. So he hit me emotionally in the 2nd week of analysis with the question of whether he could turn to my senior physician at the Sigmund-Freud-Institut (see Section 3.1.1). He said[4]:

I have to ask you a question: If I were really in distress, could I turn to the senior physician at your institute and ask for help?" I immediately registered in her countertransference most intense feelings of devaluation and attack on her psychoanalytic potency. Although I tried to control my emotions, Mr A accurately perceived this, stood up and said. "Then I will leave now—I see that I have hurt you. I'm sure you don't want to work with me now …

Only much later can we jointly understand this enactment as part of his mother's transference, who, especially during the alcoholism, has hardly been a reliable, holding object for Mr A Additionally, it turns out in the psychoanalysis, she had suffered from severe postpartum depression in the first weeks of Mr A's life. Therefore, she probably felt not able to help her baby to psychically integrate his early sadistic and destructive impulses and fantasies and to regulate his intensive affects as well as his terrible feelings of helplessness and powerlessness (see Section 3). Therefore, Mr A's own early vital libidinal and aggressive impulses had been overstimulated. They seemed to be linked to the fantasy of destroying his objects—probably one of the reasons for his psychic withdrawal and his anorectic-like coping with his body.

4.3.2   Approach to aggression and the desire
for self-agency

After about six months of psychoanalysis, the manifest dream content slowly begins to change. The dreamer is now less often alone in the dream. Other people are present. Even in terrible situations, the dreamer seems to gain at least some ability to make "autonomous" decisions, as in the following example:

> It was a very short dream. I have dreamed that I was with a friend in a room. He tells me that I have been executed. I can choose between two options choose between two options: either my head or I will be cut off or being killed by the rope that hung tightly around my neck and was pulled by a running horse. I woke up in a panic ....

Despite its terrible content, the dream shows the beginning of a process of regaining a certain control and activity in dreams, his self-agency.

In the eighth month of psychoanalysis, after Mr A had spent a night in the sleep laboratory,[5] he reported the following dream:

> I was at a party with my wife. I had to go to the restroom and found a room on another floor. I couldn't close the door and had the feeling that someone was following me. They were two men— an older and a younger one. The first one had a strange appearance. It had thick glasses on his nose and stared at me continuously. It seemed threatening. I have tried to chase him away with the toilet brush ... And then I woke up because I was actually kicked with my foot.

The associations lead to experiences of helplessness—in the sleep laboratory, where he felt unprotected, but also in the psychoanalytical sessions. Memories of scenes of complete loneliness during adolescence come up. We talk about his desire to "kick someone" instead of being "a good guy": "Well, in the dream you defend yourself with a toilet brush to protect yourself ... this seems to be an important, active step in contrast to the situation in the lab last night or here on the couch—and probably also in many situations as an adolescent where you felt like a passive victim ..." (M.LB).

4.3.3   Differentiation between self and object
representations and positive transference

He then has a series of dreams in which his chronically ill brother appears.

> In a dream, he learns that his brother is tortured. Despite his feelings of guilt because he didn't give his brother helps, he flees and brings himself in safety ...

Among other things, massive feelings of guilt became apparent at the thought of improving his professional situation, which for him would unconsciously mean that he, who is already doing so much better in his life, would now also overtake his brother professionally. After we talked about this topic, he reported the following dream:

> In my dream I was together with my brother. We were both in the same car. He drove, but he drove faster and faster and did not have the car under control. I said: I'm going to count 1,2,3 and then I take the wheel. And I have could really prevent a catastrophe ...

This is an impressive example of the successive differentiation between self and object representations (of the brother) as well as the dream subject's struggle for activity and control, his self-determination to "prevent catastrophes," his self-agency, also to better cope with his intense feelings of guilt (caused by his sadistic impulses, which were over-stimulated in his life history).

4.3.4   Grief, revenge, self-destruction,
and creativity

In the third year of psychoanalysis, the patient feels able to work most of the time and is sometimes able to resolve conflicts with colleagues in an open and productive way. He can reflect on his tendency to social withdrawal and thus counteract it. He has partially regained his creativity and enjoyment of work, although he still suffers from depressive breakdowns. This often involves his massive unconscious fears of destroying his objects through his archaic revenge impulses and aggressive fantasies. These now become directly visible in the transference, which opens a window for a deeper psychoanalytical understanding. However, aggressive impulses and thoughts continue to trigger massive fears and defense mechanisms in the patient for a long time.

This is also shown by the dreams from this period.

In a dream, people are characterized by destroyed by hurricanes. Mr A is in a panic and does not dare to see how the people lifted into the air by the hurricane and then be smashed.

Analyzing the associations to the manifest dreams reveals that the manifest dream points to the unconscious beliefs of Mr A, that his aggressive impulses will destroy his love objects and lead to unstoppable catastrophes (such as his mother's alcoholism). In psychoanalysis, it becomes understandable that the above-mentioned extremely stimulated aggressive-destructive impulses during his first months of life have also favored the development of a rigid ego-ideal and super-ego.

As we were able to work through these unconscious beliefs and fantasies in the transference, Mr A increasingly developed a sense of humor and was able to distance himself ironically from his inner demand to always be a "peaceful but inhibited analysand." In addition, he now dares to confront me more directly and risk conflicts with me, e.g. about sessions that have been missed and had to be paid. So there seems to be some evidence that the psychoanalytic treatment of this severely traumatized patient leads to a regaining of trust in a "helping inner and outer object," combined with a perceived reduction in his loneliness and an improvement in his narcissistic self-regulation and self-determination, that is, his self-agency. After a session in which we once again talk about his terrible loneliness as a teenager and how he constantly felt like a "weird bird," he starts the next session:

Mrs Bohleber—you won't believe it. I really did dream about a "weird bird": There was a large, black "weird bird" that bouncing around on the street: he really looked interesting, original and endearing. Then suddenly a sports car pulled up. Very chic young people got out of the car and looked at the bird. They wanted to take the bird with them, but I protested and did not allow them to see him. "That interesting bird is mine ..."
I said.

The associations lead to the aforementioned self-perception as a "weird bird" in his adolescence. "As a teenager, I always felt different from the others, weird, strange, not loved. I felt like I didn't belong to any of the groups at my school ... Back then, I tried to make a virtue out of necessity: I'm just different from them, so what the hell."

Motivated by our therapeutic understanding of this dream, the patient also deals with his own part in his social isolation, e.g. his arrogant contempt for his fun-loving colleagues during his military service or his angry withdrawal from his work colleagues when they once forgot to invite him to lunch. This leads to a change in his self-perception both in external reality and in the transference. As the manifest dream content (as well as the associations to the dream) may make clear, Mr A has also rediscovered his sense of humor. In dreams, this is an indicator of a growing ability of the dreaming self to establish a certain distance from emotions and thoughts and to develop a sense of control and self-agency.

Looking back on the transformation processes during psychoanalysis, the humorous creation of the "weird bird" in the above-mentioned dream was a "turning point" in the treatment: the analysand had rediscovered his sense of humor, which I also understood as an indication that he could reconnect to experiences with "good inner objects" (perhaps with his mother before her alcoholism, his father, to whom amusing memories emerge for the first time, and his grandfather, with whom he had a tender, supportive, and continuous relationship). In the terminology of the Zurich Dream Process Coding System (ZDPCS, Moser & Hortig, 2019), the model of a depressive self and object no longer completely dominated the analysand's psychic microworld (the dream scene) and dream generation, but was replaced by "embodied memories" of more adequate, less traumatic early object-relations experiences, in which positive affects and a "mobility of the self" (self-agency) were present (see e.g. Leuzinger-Bohleber, 2015). It was probably a stroke of luck in this analysis that I, as an analyst, was unconsciously able to connect to these unconscious positive object-relations experiences already during the assessment interviews with Mr A.

Let me conclude the summary of the psychoanalysis by saying that the psychic changes enable Mr A to no longer be completely inhibited in the fulfillment of his (exhibitionist) and libidinal longings and desires and to increasingly develop his creativity in his external reality, his marriage, his social relationships, as well as in his involvement in the peace movement.

I think this can also be seen in the two dreams from a night at the end of the third year of psychoanalysis, which I hope speak for themselves:

> I had two dreams last night. One was pretty funny: I was talking to the famous Jazz guitarist X. played. It went quite well and I had fun. I didn't fail and the neck of the guitar wasn't soft either (laughs).[6] The guitarist supported my improvisation and kept a low profile. Naturally I knew he was better than me, but this didn't matter—it was just fun …
>
> My wife and I observed how two men were fighting. One of them punched knocked the other one out and dragged him into the forest … We climbed onto a kind of high seat and observed everything … as in our new apartment located on the 6th floor and where we can look down … We saw how the man was holding the unconscious man into the bushes and we thought about it, to go to the police. During the dream there is a large change—we're suddenly at the police station. There are two policemen hanging around who seemed not to be interested in doing something company. In the dream, they seemed to agree to be that they will do nothing. That was very strange. We talked to them. Finally, they put on jogging bottoms and sports shoes and said they were going to have a look at all this …

4.4   Some concluding remarks

Various contemporary interdisciplinary dream models, which integrate findings from different scientific disciplines, agree that patients' nightmares can be related to (early) traumatization of the analysands. In analogy to the traumatic situation, the dream subject repeats the traumatic situation of extreme helplessness, powerlessness, and unbearable negative affects such as panic, despair, anger, and fear of death again and again—even in dreams. The dream self has lost all control over the situation and is confronted with fear of annihilation and the threat of death. As Weinstein and Ellman (2012) discuss, nightmares are triggered not only by extreme flooding anxiety, but simultaneously by the absence of a holding, containing object. As discussed in Section 3.2, trauma is defined as a situation in which the basic trust in a helping "other" and one's own ability to act is destroyed—an experience with lasting consequences (see e.g. Cooper, 1986; Bohleber, 2010). Moser and von Zeppelin (1997) postulate in their model of trauma development that traumatic complexes can be characterized by the fact that extreme affects are not "bound" (integrated) into a human relationship structure. Finally, I referred to the concept of "embodied memories" (Leuzinger-Bohleber & Pfeifer, 2002; Leuzinger-Bohleber, 2015; see also Section 3.2). As illustrated in the case study, we can find indicators of embodied memories in the manifest dreams, which imply bodily experiences in early relationships and which can often be used as indicators for a successive understanding of the (unconscious) "trauma history" of the analysand in the psychoanalytic situation.

All these different conceptualizations of dreams agree that the frequent nightmares often recounted in the early stages of psychoanalysis (including by patients in the LAC study) may indicate cumulative (early) traumatization of the analysands that eventually led to chronic depression. As I have tried to illustrate in the clinical case, Changes in the manifest dream content as well as in the association of the dream (royal pathways for understanding the latent dream content) can thus serve as signs of transformations of the inner object world, the microworlds of the analysand, during psychoanalysis. When the dream subject gains a more active attitude and control over the dangerous situation and is no longer exclusively a passive, lonely victim, but in the company of helping others, this often indicates "turning points" in the psychoanalytic process. Another indicator is the systematic change of affects in the manifest dreams: the spectrum is expanded. A single affect (such as panic) no longer dominates the dream plot as it did in the initial phase of treatment.

In the context of Chapter 1 could only illustrate, but not systematically show or theoretically discuss in detail, that in a "successful" psychoanalysis the analyst succeeds in reintegrating the (split-off) trauma with its unbearable affects and unconscious convictions into the psychoanalytic relationship. This can lead to a modification of the unconscious conviction that "nobody—but also nobody—is interested in me when I find myself in an unbearable, life-threatening situation with complete helplessness and powerlessness, without any self-determination." Of course, the traumatic experiences cannot be erased by such experiences in the transference/transference of the psychoanalytic relationship, but they can lose their quality of unbearable horror and the psychological quality of nightmares.

Therefore, changes in manifest dreams and working with dreams in the psychoanalytic situation still seem to be a "via regia to the unconscious." They are the key to understanding unconscious conflicts and fantasies and possible transformations of psychic functioning.[7]

As an analyst, of course, I do not want to simplify these transformational processes: they are never unilinear, but very complex. However, as I have tried to show in several detailed case summaries, a systematic clinical and extraclinical investigation of the changes in dreams might be a better psychoanalytic way to investigate changes in psychoanalysis or long-term psychoanalytic treatments than an exclusive investigation of symptoms.

Notes

1 An earlier version of this summary of the psychoanalysis with this patient was published in Leuzinger-Bohleber, M., & Fischmann, T. (2018). Another version will be published in Leuzinger-Bohleber et al. (in press).
2 The so called *Three Level of Clinical Observation* was developed by IPA Committee for Clinical Research with the aim of systematizing the clinical-psychoanalytic exchange among psychoanalysts as a first step towards clinical-psychoanalytic research. In the LAC study, the 3LM was used to systematically discuss the course of the psychoanalyses and the case narratives based on them in a group of experts and to prepare them for publication.
3 Mr A has agreed to publish material from his psychoanalysis. In order to maintain confidentiality, some biographical and socio-economic data have been actively altered, but without destroying the "narrative truth."
4 At that time I had been the director of this psychoanalytic research institute (see e.g. Leuzinger-Bohleber & Plänkers, 2019).
5 Because most of the patients in the LAC Depression Study suffered from severe sleeping disturbances, we had the chance to study their sleep (and dreams) also in the sleeping laboratory and check the possibility of (temporary) medication by an experimental sleep researcher and psychiatrist.
6 Mr A refers here to a dream he had told the week before. After a quarrel with his wife he had erection problems and then slept from a guitar with a "soft neck."
7 Our research group is therefore currently developing its own dream transformation scale to systematically test the hypotheses outlined above using around 60 dream diaries of patients from the MODE study. In doing so, we are trying to alleviate a dilemma faced by analysts who engage in empirical psychotherapy research, in which we have to fulfill the criteria of evidence-based medicine so that our studies—e.g. by health insurance companies—are taken seriously. Therefore, in the design of the MODE study, we tried to use instruments that are closer to psychoanalysis in addition to psychological and neuroscientific measurement instruments: These include the analysis of changes in the dream diaries of our analysands (see e.g. Leuzinger-Bohleber et al., (2023)).

References

Bohleber, W. (2010). *Was Psychoanalyse Heute Leistet. Identität Und Intersubjektivität, Trauma Und Therapie, Gewalt Und Gesellschaft*, Stuttgart: Klett-Cotta. In English (not identical publication): Bohleber, W. (2012). *Destructiveness, Intersubjectivity, and Trauma: The Identity Crisis of Modern Psychoanalysis*. London: Karnac.

Cooper, A. M. (1986). Toward a limited definition of psychic trauma. In A. Rothstein (Ed.), *The Reconstruction of Trauma: Its Significance in Clinical Work* (pp. 41–56). Madison, CT: International Universities Press, Inc.

De Leon de Bernardi, B., & Leuzinger-Bohleber, M. (2021). The 3-LM's contribution to developments in analytic treatment. In M. A. Fitzpatrick Hanly, M. Altman de Litvan, & R. Bernardi (Eds.), *Change Through Time in Psychoanalysis* (pp. 211–234). London: Karnac.

Leuzinger-Bohleber, M. (2015). *Finding the Body in the Mind—Embodied Memories, Trauma, and Depression*. London: Karnac: International Psychoanalytical Association.

Leuzinger-Bohleber, M., & Fischmann, T. (2018). Neuroscientifically inspired psychoanalysis: Chronic depression as a paradigmatical example. In H. Boeker, P. Hartwich, & G. Northoff (Eds.), *Neuropsychodynamic Psychiatry* (pp. 579–597). Cham: Springer. https://doi.org/10.1007/978-3-319-75112-2_29

Leuzinger-Bohleber, M., & Pfeifer, R. (2002). Remembering a depressive primary object? Memory in the dialogue between psychoanalysis and cognitive science. *International Journal of Psychoanalysis*, *83*, 3–33.

Leuzinger-Bohleber, M., & Plänkers, T. (2019). The struggle for a psychoanalytic research institute: The evolution of frankfurts sigmund-freud-institute. *International Journal of Psychoanalysis*, *100*(5), 962–987.

Leuzinger-Bohleber, M., Grabhorn, A., & Bahrke, U. (Eds.) (2020). *What can Only Be Told and Not Measured*. Gießen: Psychosozial-Verlag.

Leuzinger-Bohleber, M., Donié, M., Wichelmann, J., Ambresin, G., & Fischmann, T. (2023). Changes in dreams – On the development of a dream-transformation scale in psychoanalyses with chronically depressed, early traumatized patients. Accepted for publication by *The Scandinavian Psychoanalytic Review*, 46:1–2, 82–93. doi:10.1080/01062301.2023.2297116.

Moser, U., & Hortig, V. (2019). *Mikrowelt Traum: Affektregulierung Und Reflexion*. Frankfurt a.M: Brandes & Apsel.

Moser, U., & von Zeppelin, I. (1997). *Der Geträumte Traum: Wie Träume Entstehen Und Sich Verändern*. Stuttgart: Kohlhammer.

Weinstein, L., & Ellmann, S. (2012). Traumforschung in der psychoanalyse: Klinische studien, traumserien, extraklinische forschung im labor. *Psyche–Z Psychanal*, *66*, 833–861.

Chapter 5

Depression in the life span of depressed individuals

Some considerations concerning specific challenges in psychoanalytic treatments

As mentioned in the introduction, depression can occur at any age, which must, of course, be taken into account in psychoanalytic treatment, as we have also explained in the treatment manual as well as in numerous psychoanalytic publications (Leuzinger-Bohleber, Fischmann & Beutel, 2022, pp. 79–86, see also e.g. McGinley & Varchevker, 2010). In this chapter, therefore, we can refer to these publications and restrict ourselves to just a few considerations and case examples. They will be used to briefly point out that both the understanding of the psychodynamics of depression and its treatment must always be reflected on a developmental-psychological background that takes into account the specific tasks in the respective life cycle, as Erik Erikson (1971) already postulated in his epigenetic model of psychosocial development (Stufenmodell der psychosozialen Entwicklung). Each stage of development—from infancy to old age—corresponds to characteristic developmental tasks that can be mastered through the acquisition of skills. In relation to the first year of life, Erikson spoke of the two poles of *basic trust versus basic mistrust,* for adolescence of *identity versus identity diffusion* and for adulthood of *generativity versus stagnation and self-absorption.*

There is a broad psychoanalytic literature, which discusses, for example, specific treatment options for depression in babies, preschool children, primary school children, and adolescents, as well as patients in old age. We can, therefore, limit ourselves here to briefly mentioning treatment with depressed patients in developmental stages, which are of special interest for this volume: very young children (Section 5.1), of patients in so-called emerging adulthood (Section 5.2) and patients in

DOI: 10.4324/9781003455349-5

adulthood for illustrating the importance of the transgenerational perspective of psychoanalysis with patients (as e.g. Mr A) (Section 5.3).

5.1   *Basic trust versus basic mistrust*: Psychoanalytic therapies for chronically depressed patients in early childhood

It is now undisputed that even *babies* can have depressive reactions or
even develop serious depression, as already the famous hospitalization
studies of René Spitz in the 1940th have shown (Spitz, 1946). Many
psychoanalytical studies have been very influential see e.g. Daniel
Stern (2010/1985) and many of the contributions in the Volume "Early
Parenting and Prevention of Disorder. Psychoanalytic Research at Interdisciplinary Frontiers," edited by Robert Emde and me in 2014: e.g.
Massimo Ammaniti et al., Daniel Schechter et al., Antoine Guedeney
et al., Henri Parens, Agneta Sandell, Kai von Klitzing, Patrick Meurs,
to mention just a few.

At two Sandler conferences, we studied this topic from different
perspectives: *Research in Early Parenting and the Prevention of Disorder, Interdisciplinary Challenges and Opportunities* 2012 (published
by Emde & Leuzinger-Bohleber, 2014) and *Finding the Body in the
Mind. Researchers and Clinicians in Dialogue* 2013 (published by
Leuzinger-Bohleber, Emde & Pfeifer, 2013). In particular, some consequences for the therapy of babies and their families as well as for
early prevention were pointed out. To mention just one example:

Agneta Sandell (2014) presented an impressive psychoanalytic
treatment under the title "From nameless dread to bearable fear:
the psychoanalytic treatment of a twenty-two-month-old child"
(pp. 328–342). The mother reported that little Hilda "never
seemed to be calm and secure, never peaceful, not even in the
presence of her mother ... (between) six to seven months ... it
was possible to put her down without her screaming, but she just
lay there, staring into nothingness as it seemed" (p. 329). The
child had withdrawn into herself and showed severe early depression. Sandell discusses that this was related to early trauma
during and shortly after her birth. The mother had almost died

when Hilda was born and had to stay in hospital for several weeks. The father was in shock and utterly distressed. He felt completely powerless and terrified and could barely cope with the baby and his 11-month-old brother on his own.

Sandell describes her psychoanalytic work in detail and shows impressively how she was able to help Hilda out of his depressive withdrawal and, using the language of the child, make her understand the early traumatization she had suffered and her unconscious fantasies associated with it. Together with the intensive work with both parents, the child was led out of the threatening mental state during the 10 months of intensive psychoanalytical therapy. Hilda developed into a cheerful, lively and expressive toddler who was able to catch up on many of her missed developmental processes, e.g. in terms of language, but also in terms of her social skills, and resume the interrupted developmental path.

Such therapeutic experiences have motivated psychoanalysts for decades to become involved in therapies with babies and toddlers as well as in early prevention (see Chapter 7).

5.2 *Identity versus identity-diffusion*: Specific challenges in psychoanalyses with chronic depressed patients in the so-called "emerging adulthood"[1]

An increasing number of patients, between 20 and 30, with severe depression are looking for help in the psychoanalytic outdoor clinic in Frankfurt a.M. Some of them suffer from an almost complete arrest of their psychic development, often connected with a depressive breakdown. For years, this age group has had the highest prevalence rates for mental disorders, specifically depression, viewed over a lifetime (Jacobi et al., 2014).

Some of these patients were interested in participating in the MODE study (see Section 1.3). A special feature of this study is that, for methodological and professional ethical reasons, analysts and analysands decide after one year of treatment whether and with what weekly session frequency they would like to continue psychoanalysis. In this framework, we made unexpected clinical observations. Surprisingly, the young patients of the study mostly reacted very positively to this special feature of the setting: "I think it is good that I can have the possibility to decide after a year. I would like to begin psychoanalysis, but it is inconceivable to me to commit myself to several years. One year is manageable, then we'll see ..." (Mrs U, 23-year-old student). We understood such attitudes primarily as an indicator of a fear of dependence, which is, as discussed e.g. by Bohleber (2017), often related to the inner and outer separation process from the primary objects. A new (fantasized and partially real) dependence on the psychoanalyst is experienced as threatening to their own process of identity finding and stabilization in this developmental phase of life. These inner fears and conflicts are also often interwoven with demands in the outside world. A great deal of flexibility is demanded of young people in many contemporary training programs and professions: for example, experience abroad is one of the important qualifying features for a future career in many fields.—These are all parts of the reasons why some psychoanalysts hesitate to offer high-frequency psychoanalysis to patients in this age group, as it is feared that it will encourage treatment drop-out (see also argumentation by Abend, 1987). Instead, low-frequency psychotherapy or brief therapy is recommended.

As we have discussed in another paper with the help of a detailed case study, there seems to be a third possibility, namely to offer these patients intensive, but limited psychoanalysis in terms of the total duration (Leuzinger-Bohleber, 2023). These patients may overcome their developmental standstill with the help of intensive psychoanalysis. Metaphorically speaking, their psychoanalyses help to make their lame wings vibrate again and become fledglings, already after around one year of psychoanalysis, although, of course, the analytic process is not yet completed. If such psychoanalytic experiences are experienced as helpful, this might be decisive for these seriously ill young adults in motivating them to continue their psychoanalyses, even after an interruption forced, for example, due to stays abroad, and thus to prevent chronification of their depression or a spillover to other mental illnesses.

This was the case for many of the 48% of all the 110 patients in emerging adulthood which underwent psychoanalysis in the frame of the MODE study until the end of 2023. Mr X was one of them, who, with the help of his psychoanalysis, was able to overcome his complete standstill of the individuation/separation process in his emerging adulthood. After only

15 months of highly frequent psychoanalysis, he was able to go abroad and finish his studies, although the psychoanalytic process obviously had been limited. After two years abroad, he came back to the analyst and continued his psychoanalysis for several more months. Here is a short summary of his psychoanalysis (for more details, see Leuzinger-Bohleber, 2023).

> Mr X, a 24 year-old student, was in an extremely vulnerable mental and psychosocial state when he was sent to psycho-analytic treatment by his psychiatrist after a serious suicidal attempt. His mental development had come to a complete stand-still. He had withdrawn into an autistic-like shell, spent his days depressed in bed at his parent's house, had dropped out of his studies and had hardly any social contacts. In the sessions (once a week), bridging the time until the highly frequent psychoa-nalysis could start, I had great doubts about being able to reach the patient psychoanalytically at all. Looking back on this psy-choanalysis, I have the impression that a high-frequency setting (first three, then four weekly sessions) was necessary to break the patient's developmental blockade: an intensive transference relationship developed, which made it possible to address and work through the patient's aggressive-destructive impulses and fantasies rather directly, already as part of the transference, at an early stage of the treatment. On the basis of impressive dreams, it became apparent how much the boundaries between self and object representations, pregenital and Oedipal fantasies and con-flicts, as well as the barriers between generations and genders, had merged in the inner object world of the patient. This was obvious in the very first dream he had reported during treatment:
>
>> I dreamt of a man who had his own clinic. He was in the gar-den, looked terrible—very big (all the proportions were not right). He had a terrible disease: the upper body was huge, the lower part of the body was like a cone, with a sinister surface. I cannot describe this at all. Do you know black spi-ders that carry their children on their backs? This is what this looked like. Spider threads were all around him, I wanted to help the man, but I didn't know how. I also couldn't diag-nose what was wrong with him.

These psychic realities became successively accessible in the psychoanalytic process and could be worked through successively. As is well known, such mental differentiation processes always take place simultaneously in the external world as well as in the transference relationship. These processes could be observed in an impressive way in this psychoanalysis. Encouraged by the analytic work, he dared to postpone his final university examination date against his mother's will, to move out of the parental home and to plan a stay abroad. These changes in the outside reality had an enormous influence on the psychic and psychosocial situation of the patient, as well as on transformations in his inner object world. To mention just one example: Success with passing the exam and leaving home led to new narcissistic gratifications and new social relationships in the outside world, which strengthened his fragile self-esteem and his autonomy and encouraged him to turn to new objects. At the same time, it was essential to work through central unconscious fantasies connected with the separation and identity-finding processes, mobilizing homicidal, and suicidal impulses in the transference, probably unconscious sources of Mr X's severe depressive breakdown. As Winnicott (1971) described it a long time ago, the survival of the object (the analyst in the transference) was essential for coping with the archaic aggressive-destructive fantasies and impulses as well as with the immense guilt feelings connected with them.

From a treatment point of view, the handling of the serious conflicts in connection with the separation and individuation processes of Mr X was particularly demanding. My first association: "He doesn't feel at home in his body ..." probably hit the bull's eye: Mr X's body unconsciously still belonged to the mother and was, therefore, the object of archaic destructive impulses and fantasies, as well as a deep refusal to renounce infantile longings and desires and to give up the self-image of a "sexless" infant to be nurtured and held. As a result of the traumatogenic pathological object relationship, self-agency, as well as primal trust in a helping, empathic object, had collapsed: the flight into a passive "dead" dissociative inner state was part of unconscious revenge against the depressed, psychologically abusive primary object: a central unconscious fantasy of the patient was that he was *caught in the poisoned web and could not escape the greedy sucking spider anyway*, and therefore turned the passively feared into an active "fact" himself: he transformed himself into an empty, dead shell in which no life could be found anymore. We also discovered another important unconscious fantasy of himself being a "spherical man" (Aristophanes, see Manuwald, 2013), both man and woman, with penis and vagina, who can satisfy himself without depending on anyone for the satisfaction of his desires and longings. Connected to this was a sadistic triumph, a fantasy of revenge on his objects, since no one managed to really help him and put him out of his misery. It was important to understand not only the regressive quality of these fantasies but also the progressive impulse to gain autonomy and become less dependent on the (primary) objects.

Discovering these unconscious fantasies and working through the life-threatening conflicts and impulses in the transference relationship was the prerequisite for breaking through the developmental blockade and restarting the self- and identity-finding process of emerging adulthood. Psychoanalysis could help the patient to stabilize the inner boundaries between self and object representations, fantasy and reality, but also between generations—a prerequisite for developing a more stable basic sense of his own self.

5.3 *Generativity versus stagnation and self-absorption*: Psychoanalyses in adulthood trying to interrupt the transgenerational transmission of trauma

About one-third of the chronically depressed patients in the MODE study have been more than 40 years old. For many of them, a so-called mid-life crisis had been one reason for starting a psychoanalysis. There were many reasons for such crises. To pick out just a few aspects: for some patients, it was a mid-life career adjustment that exacerbated the depression. For quite a great number of women, the worsening of their depression is linked to menopause and the feeling of having to say goodbye to the biologically fertile phase of life as a woman, an aspect that has been relatively little discussed in the psychoanalytical literature to date (see e.g. Leuzinger-Bohleber, 2001).

For others, it was relationship crises or an increased suffering from social isolation[2]. For many of the patients, as for Mr A (see Section 4), the midlife crisis seemed to be related to the collapse of the sense of time due to the traumatization suffered (see Section 3.2). In the fourth or fifth decade of their lives, they were confronted with the fact that they were somehow not actively living their lives. "I never really arrived in life ..." said Mr U in one of the assessment interviews. Psychoanalysis at this age often serves to help the patients face the painful reality that possibly half of their lives have already passed and to regain their own self-agency so that they can actively take control of their own lives.

Another aspect should be briefly highlighted here using the following short case study as an example. Some chronically depressed patients seek psychoanalytic help because they unconsciously fear to pass on their own misery to their children. In fact, as already briefly mentioned, for many of the former patients of the Follow-Up Study of the German Psychoanalytic Association and the comparative depression study (LAC study), the most important result of their psychoanalyses was that they were able to cut the unconscious umbilical cord of traumatization. The brief summary of psychoanalysis with Mr H may serve as an illustration of this complex issue

Mr H had been suffering from major depression for 25 years and belonged to the group of patients for whom short therapies and most psychotropic drugs did not seem to help and whose depressive episodes recurred at increasingly shorter intervals and became worse and worse.

Mr H is the only child of his parents. About his early history it is known that he was a "cry baby." The parents were obviously very helpless and went to a pediatrician who advised them not to pay attention to the baby and to let him cry ... This would strengthen the lungs ... The mother suffered from pronounced obsessive-compulsive symptomatology (see also Leuzinger-Bohleber et al., 2017). The father also complained of a range of psychosomatic symptoms and had experienced a "nervous breakdown" in a stressful situation at work.

Mr H comes from what is in many respects a "typical German family of the 20th century." Both parents experienced World War II as teenagers and still vividly remember how they suffered as children under the rigid National Socialist educational ideology. One of his grandfathers had lost an arm in the First World War. He had a violent temper and often beat the children brutally.

Mr H's mother had to undergo an appendectomy when the patient was 4 years old. For this reason, her son was sent to a children's recreation home for several weeks, which was apparently run according to pedagogical principles that still dated from the Nazi era. In psychoanalysis, H. found out what a traumatic experience the stay at the home had been for him. In psychoanalysis, it becomes clear that due to the traumatic separation from his love objects, he had largely lost the basic trust in his inner objects and self-agency and lived for years in a dissociative state. In many dreams of the initial phase of psychoanalysis, he experiences himself in mortal danger, alone and full of panic, fear and despair. Here is just one example:

> I see a badly injured man lying on the side of the road—his guts are hanging out and there's blood everywhere. A helicopter appears. It is still unclear if the man is being shot at or if he is being helped. Someone shows up and claims the man is dead. I notice that the man is still alive and that he opens his eyes and says, 'Why is no one coming to help me?' A woman hands him the lid of a cooking pot to put over the wound. ... I awake in a state of panic.
>
> (Leuzinger-Bohleber, 2015a, p. 2; see also Section 4.1)

Despite the dissociative mental states and his social isolation, Mr H was a good student, first completing an apprenticeship and later a university degree. In adolescence, he had a psychosomatic breakdown, which his parents diagnosed as a growth crisis and tried to help him with a vitamin cure. At the age of 15, he found his first girlfriend. His condition improved. But when he broke up with her at the age of 22, this triggered—completely unexpectedly for him—severe psychosomatic reactions.

When his girlfriends later broke up, these intensified until he finally suffered a dramatic breakdown at a party in honor of a new girlfriend: he had to be admitted to the hospital for hyperventilation (panic attack).

At the beginning of psychoanalysis, he was married to a woman from a non-European country and had a 3 ½ year old son. The last severe depression (2 ½ years ago) had been triggered when his wife, in a physical and psychological state of exhaustion after months of a double burden of renovating their apartment, coldly and violently accused him of endangering his son's life because he had crawled toward an open paint can. Mr H could not defend himself against this attack. The next morning, he awoke with a severe, unbearable depression.

The son was literally lying on the couch with him. Impressively, it was the patient's relationship with his son that showed his analyst after 3 months that psychoanalysis was having an impact on Mr H. The first weeks of treatment were marked by violent, aggressive-destructive conflicts in his marriage. The young son was often exposed to extremely aggressive conflicts between the parents. The dynamics of the first weeks filled me with great concern and doubt as to whether psychoanalysis could really reach into Mr H's inner world. To my amazement, however, after three months of treatment, Mr H was able to get his son, now almost four years old, to sit on the potty and do without a diaper, an indication to me that Mr H could somehow use psychoanalysis to strengthen his paternal functions. At this point, his son seemed to represent a kind of self-object of the patient: In the child's panic and desperate crying, Mr H often recognized his own affects as a child and, at the same time, sought the experience of being able to comfort and reassure the little one, an incipient attempt to distinguish between his infantile, traumatized self and the adult self (see, among others, Seiffge-Krenke & Weitkamp, 2020).

When his wife left him and his son after 3 months of treatment because of a sexual affair, he was flooded with panic and despair, could hardly sleep and needed his parents to take care of his son. Surprisingly, the child came to rest during those weeks and, according to the kindergarten teachers, developed positively: he overcame his selective mutism and gently began to find his way out of his social isolation.

The process of differentiation between self and object representation seemed to develop continuously. Around the middle of the second year of treatment, Mr H related the following dream:

> We were on a walk in the forest. A kind of teddy bear accompanied us. Suddenly the bear turned into a dangerous lion. I grabbed the son and fled. The lion followed us. At the last moment I found shelter in a doghouse—I barely fit in …

The associations showed that he fled together with his son into the "children's hut" and "left the wife to be eaten by the lion"—a dream image that Mr H could place in connection with his desire for revenge and death to his wife (but also to his primary objects and to me as a transference figure). The dream image again contained the lack of inner separation from his son, who at this point still seems to be predominantly an infantile alter ego or a narcissistic self-object of the analysand.

In the course of the treatment, the inner boundaries between him and his son gradually stabilize. I had the impression that this makes it possible to increasingly free the son from transgenerational repetition compulsion. Although Mr H has—consciously—always protected the son from separations in order not to subject him to a similar separation trauma as he experienced himself, he could only insufficiently develop a trialogue with his baby and his mother and thus support him as an early triangulating object or later in the oedipal phase when separating from the maternal primary object. This was probably one of the reasons why his son—like the patient—developed into a dreamy, socially withdrawn, anxious, and latency child.

Crucial to psychological development was, among other things, recognizing and bearing ambivalent feelings toward his objects—In the third year of treatment, the patient recounted a frightening nightmare in which he saw his son's body floating by in an aquarium. The associations led to his death wishes toward his son. "Without him, I could have divorced my wife a long time ago and started a new life—sometimes I feel as dependent on him as I must have felt as a small child on my parents who put me in a home ..."

Another dream from the third year of psychoanalysis illustrates the inner transformations of his relationship with his son:

> I went to the kindergarten. There were many children there—a warm, lively atmosphere. A boy was sitting on my lap—we were joking with each other, the way men do with each other. I gave him a hug. To my surprise, it was not my son, it was another boy. My son's teacher was also present. He was full of admiration as he watched me—I was very happy. But suddenly I looked closer at the boy and saw bugs and a black spider crawling out of his eyes—it was horrible, scary and threatening, the boy was completely transformed. He looked pale and sick and had deep dark circles under his eyes.—I was shocked and woke up in a panic.

His first association was, "The eyes are the window to the soul ..." Then he remembered his wife's abrupt mood swings. A few weeks ago, after much hesitation, he finally sought out a public child guidance center because his son, now almost 10 years old, was still sleeping in his mother's bed. He himself had been unable to set limits on his wife's overwhelming and seductive behavior. The counselor described his wife as a borderline personality because she could change from a charming, gentle woman to an angry, shrieking, violent witch who lost control of herself and her affects from one moment to the next.

> And in her dream, a relaxed, happy atmosphere suddenly turns into a threatening, horrible and repulsive situation—the normal, lovable boy mutates into a very sick child. Could it be that you are subconsciously worried that your son might become as sick as your wife?" (Analyst). Mr H was silent before he finally said, "At the same time, I think that the boy in the dream could also be a part of me ... Suddenly I am

overwhelmed by my unbearable chronic whole body pain
and feel like a miserable, seriously ill and helpless child ...

In the following sessions, we cautiously approached the hith-
erto unbearable inner truth that not only was his wife seriously
ill and often lost control over herself and her affects, but that
he himself carried an analogous, threatening, sinister, and dangerous inner world within himself, harboring black spiders and
hideous insects. Gradually it became possible to recognize and
understand the projections and projective identifications in his
relationship with his wife—and also with the analyst. Only now
was it possible for Mr H to perceive his own archaic impulses
and death wishes toward women, which had often appeared in
his dreams, and to integrate them psychologically, at least in
part (cf. Leuzinger-Bohleber, 2015a).

*Some further remarks on the transgenerational transmission
of trauma*

The regular high-frequency psychoanalysis ended after a good
five years. Since the marital situation deteriorated dramatically
shortly after the end of the psychoanalysis, we agreed on another
weekly telephonic session, which enabled me to receive regular
information about the further development of Mr H and his son.

A few summary remarks on this:

The marital relationship sometimes reminded me of a com-
municating tube: The more stable Mr H felt, the more unstable his wife became. She increasingly developed the image
of a manifest borderline personality. Again, there were frequent scenes of violence: Finally, Mrs H. attacked her husband with a knife, so that he called the police. Mrs H. was
admitted to the psychiatric hospital. Finally, she was ready to
take medication. In the following weeks, Mr H's self-esteem
was determined by his ability to cope with "real life with a
child." "I'm no longer that little kid who completely breaks
down without his mother and can't get anything done ..."

The actual separation from his sick mother led to an impressive development of the son. He overcame the secondary

enuresis he had suffered from for a year, a symptom that had strikingly increased his shyness, his social withdrawal, and his retreat into an increasingly dangerous computer game addiction. This was related, in my opinion, to his mother's difficulty in extricating him from a pathological relationship with her. Mr H's helplessness to support his son in his separation process from his primary object was probably another reason for the transgenerational transmission of his separation trauma to his son—so that now—six years after the beginning of his psychoanalysis—Mr H's observation of his son's progressive development was an important motive to initiate the divorce despite severe feelings of guilt and the still massive separation anxiety. The wife was admitted to a psychiatric institution and cared for by social workers and psychiatrists. The youth welfare office offered the son play therapy in combination with regular talks with his parents.

This support facilitated the son's transition to a very demanding high school. Despite initial difficulties, especially with his classmates, he was able to master school and showed increasingly better academic performance. This led to a surprisingly good coping with puberty and a visible stabilization of his self-esteem. Together with his father, he regularly visited his mentally ill mother, but he showed a clear outer (and presumably at the same time inner) separation from her.

It was impressive how he turned his threatening computer game addiction into a part of his adolescent identity development: he participated in nationwide competitions for a specific computer game, achieved success, socialized with peers, and developed autonomous skills (e.g. traveling on his own, organizing competitions on his own, etc.) (see, e.g. Lemma, 2010).

As a 15-year-old, he had expressed to his father his own vision of his future: he wanted to become rich (unlike his father, who was constantly having financial difficulties). A few weeks later, he decided to give up his gambling addiction altogether and devote himself to an alternative "scientific project" instead. In order to become rich, but also "to save the world," he had the idea of using hurricanes to generate alternative electricity.

These visions of the future bear the traits of a "normal" adolescent identity-finding process, which, on the one hand, is still characterized by fantasies of omnipotence but, on the other hand, is definitely connected with the attempt to integrate specific talents and competencies, impulses to distance oneself from primary objects, and one's own visions inspired by peers. Moreover, despite the divorce of his parents and their mental illnesses and vulnerabilities, the adolescent son of Mr H was able to use the revival of Oedipal fantasies and conflicts in early adolescence to detach himself from Oedipal objects in external, but presumably also in internal reality, and to stabilize the boundaries between self and object representation.

This development of the son relieved Mr H very much:

> Without the possibility to understand and process my separation trauma in psychoanalysis, I would hardly have been able to let go of my son internally. Moreover, a divorce from my wife would not have been possible … perhaps my son would then have become as mentally ill as his mother … he said.

Notes

1 Due to the changed status of adolescence in developmental theory, the phase of young adulthood is also undergoing a different evaluation. In the classical conceptions, the adolescent developmental processes took place between the ages of 10/11 and 20/21. After that came the period of post-adolescence or young adulthood, without assigning it the character of a developmental phase. It was rather understood as a short period of transition to the adult autonomous personality (see e.g. Blos, 1954, 1967; Freud, 1958/1965; Erikson, 1968/1971 and Laufer & Laufer, 1984). The structural changes in society that have been taking place for about the last 50 years have led to rapid economic and technical developments in the Western world. This has objectively expanded the individual's options for action, but at the same time has liquefied or even dissolved previously valid stable identity-guiding orientation schemes. *Lifestyles have become enormously pluralized and gender roles have changed dramatically and become more flexible.* As a result, a historically new age status has been established, a still-youth phase that is no longer biologically but socially regulated. It was defined already in the 1982 Shell Youth Study as a phase in which the adolescent does not

cross over into adulthood, but becomes independent in social, intellectual and sexual terms without being economically self-sufficient. This phase can extend beyond the third decade of life. Psychology and the social sciences have elaborately studied this newly defined structured period of life in recent decades. Based on his research, psychologist Jeffrey Arnett (2000) conceptualized a new developmental phase he called "emerging adulthood," characterized by greater personal freedom, as well as social and psychological experimentation, making it enormously heterogeneous. It is the most volatile phase in human life. The image of adulthood for young adults is no longer oriented around the completion of education and planning a career, or marriage and parenthood, but around certain character traits. For them, adulthood means: 1. taking responsibility for one's own self, and 2. being able to make independent decisions. In the meantime, the characteristic five features described by Arnett as typical (self-focus, delay in identity, instability, feeling in between, diversity) have been found in numerous studies with young people in many Western industrialized nations (Arnett, 2015). This makes it clear that identity formation has become the central task of this developmental phase and has thus moved away from the period of late adolescence and into the period of young adulthood.).

2 One finding of the LAC study is important in this context: 50% of the 252 patients were single and had no children.

References

Abend, S. (1987). Evaluating young adults for analysis. *Psychoanalytic Inquiry*, *7*, 31–38.

Arnett, J. J. (2000). Emerging adulthood. A theory of development from the late teens through the twenties. *American Psychologist*, *200*, 469–480.

Arnett, J. J. (Ed.) (2015). *The Oxford Handbook of Emerging Adulthood*. New York: Oxford University Press.

Blos, P. (1954). Prolonged adolescence: The formulation of a syndrome and its Therapeutic implications. *American Journal of Orthopsychiatry*, *24*, 733–742.

Blos, P. (1967). The second individuation process in adolescence. *Psychoanalytic Study of the Child*, *22*, 162–187.

Bohleber, W. (2017). *Spätadoleszenz und junges Erwachsenenalter in der heutigen Zeit. Konzeptuelle und behandlungstechnische Überlegungen*. Unpublished keynote lecture given at the conference: Adolescence in a World of Risks. Frankfurt a.M., March 3–5, 2017.

Emde, R. N., & Leuzinger-Bohleber, M. (Eds.) (2014). *Early Parenting and Prevention of Disorder: Psychoanalytic Research at Interdisciplinary Frontiers*. London: Karnac.

Erikson, E. H. (1968/1971). *Identity, Youth and Crisis*. New York: W. W. Norton.

Erikson, E. H. (1971). *Childhood and Society* [1950]. Stuttgart: Klett-Cotta (German fourth edition).

Freud, A. (1958/1965). *Normality and Psychopathology in Childhood*. New York: International University Press.

Jacobi, F., Höfler, M., Strehle, J., Mack, S., Gerschler, A., Scholl, L., Busch, M. A., Maske, U., Hapke, U., Gaebel, W., Maier, W., Wagner, M., Zielasek, J., & Wittchen, H. U. (2014). *Psychische Störungen in der Allgemeinbevölkerung: Studie zur Gesundheit Erwachsener in Deutschland und ihr Zusatzmodul Psychische Gesundheit* (DEGS1-MH).

Laufer, M., & Laufer, E. (1984). *Adolescence and Developmental Breakdown*. New Haven/London: Yale Universities Press.

Lemma, A. (2010). An order of pure decision: Growing up in a virtual world and the adolescent's experience of being-in-a-body. *Journal of the American Psychoanalytic Association, 58*(4), 691–714. https://doi.org/10.1177/0003065110385576

Leuzinger-Bohleber, M. (2001). The 'Medea fantasy'. An unconscious determinant of psychogenic sterility. *The International Journal of Psychoanalysis, 82*, 323–345.

Leuzinger-Bohleber, M. (2015a, June). Working with severely traumatized, chronically depressed analysands. *The International Journal of Psychoanalysis, 96*(3), 611–636.

Leuzinger-Bohleber, M. (2023). "Il fili di ragno lo circondavano" Lánalisi'ad alte frequenza' è una buona scelta per gli arresti evolutivi nello "stato adulto emergente"? *Rivista di Psicoanalisi, LXIX*(2), 1–26.

Leuzinger-Bohleber, M., Emde, R. N., & Pfeifer, R. (Eds.) (2013). *Embodiment: ein innovatives Konzept für Entwicklungsforschung und Psychoanalyse*. Göttingen: Vandenhoeck & Ruprecht.

Leuzinger-Bohleber, M., Fischmann, T., & Beutel, M. E. (2022). *Chronische Depression. Psychoanalytische Langzeittherapie*. Reihe: Praxis der psychodynamischen Psychotherapie—analytische und tiefenpsychologisch fundierte Psychotherapie, Bd. 12. Göttingen: Hogrefe Verlag.

Leuzinger-Bohleber, M., Kallenbach, L., Asseburg, L., Lebiger-Vogel, J., & Rickmeyer, C. (2017). Psychoanalytische Fokaltherapien für Patienten mit Zwangsstörungen? *Psyche—Z Psychoanal, 71*(98), 704–732. https://doi.org/10.21706/ps-71-8-704

Manuwald, B. (2013). *6 Die Rede des Aristophanes (189a1–193e2)* (pp. 89–104). Berlin: Akademie Verlag.

McGinley, E., & Varchevker, A. (Eds.) (2010). *Enduring Loss: Mourning, Depression and Narcissism Throughout the Life Cycle*. London: Routledge. https://doi.org/10.4324/9780429474248

Sandell, A. (2014). From nameless dread to bearable fear: The psychoanalytic treatment of a twenty-two-month-old child. In R. N. Emde & M. Leuzinger-Bohleber (Eds.), *Early Parenting and Prevention of Disorder: Psychoanalytic Research at Interdisciplinary Frontiers* (pp. 328–342). London: Karnac.

Seiffge-Krenke, I., & Weitkamp, K. (2020). How individual coping, mental health, and parental behavior is related to identity development in emerging adults in seven countries. *Emerging Adulthood 8*(5), 344–360. https://doi.org/10.1177/2167696819863504

Spitz, R. A. (1946). Hospitalism: A follow-up report on investigation described in volume I, 1945. *The Psychoanalytic Study of the Child, 2*(1), 113–117.

Stern, D. N. (2010 [1985]). *The infant's Life Experience*. With a new introduction by the author. Translated by W. Krege, edited by E. Vorspohl. 10th ed. Stuttgart: Klett-Cotta.

Winnicott, D. W. (1971). *Playing and Reality*. New York: Basic Books, Inc.

Chapter 6

Psychoanalytical depression research in interdisciplinary exchange

Some few remarks

As discussed in the introduction, depression is considered a polymorphic, heterogeneous disease in contemporary psychoanalysis. Psychoanalysis shares this view with many other scientific disciplines, as Jiménez, Botto and Fonagy (2021), among others, elaborate in their book *Etiopathogenic Theory and Models in Depression*. In it, they combine psychoanalytic, psychiatric, neurobiological, genetic, etiological, socio-psychological, and cultural perspectives on this modern, widespread Illness. The authors pronounce that psychoanalysis can be an important voice in the interdisciplinary dialogue, emphasizing the importance of unconscious fantasies and conflicts in the development of depression. At the same time, psychoanalysts in multidisciplinary teams gain access to research findings and theories from other disciplines that can complement, expand or possibly modify the psychoanalytic understanding of depression.

I can, therefore, refer here to this overview of the state of interdisciplinary research in this highly readable, up-to-date overview and limit myself to just briefly mentioning two areas of research that seem particularly important for the argumentation in this volume.

They seem to be considered only relatively rarely in clinical discussions: a) evolutionary biology and b) genetics and epigenetics

a) There are interesting convergences between central clinical-psychoanalytical observations with severely depressed patients and some of today's *evolutionary-biological views*. These describe various consequences that have resulted from a solution to an evolutionary dilemma with far-reaching consequences for humans. Because the neocortex proved to be a survival advantage in the course of evolution, birth became a threatening event for mother and child due to the large head of the foetus. Therefore, evolution found the

DOI: 10.4324/9781003455349-6

compromise of a psychophysiological premature birth. In contrast to other mammals, humans experience early development up to autonomous locomotion extrauterine. A calf can stand on its own two feet just a few hours after birth. A human baby needs about a year to take its first steps. Therefore, the evolutionary solution just mentioned is associated with the basic experience of immobility, powerlessness and existential dependence on primary objects, which is now one major focus in a contemporary psychoanalytic perspective on depression (see Section 3). However, it is well known that there are also great advantages to this evolutionary solution, e.g. that the enormous neoplasticity of the human infant can be enormously stimulated by favorable environmental conditions in these first months of life.

In connection with this human condition, Panksepp (2004), for example, postulated that millions of years ago, the bond to the mother animal and specific reactions to separation from it proved to be a survival advantage. Mark Solms (2022) describes how this evolutionary-biological superiority was reflected in the development of the human brain and linked to depressive affects:

> In light of such commonplace observations to the effect that depressive feelings are connected with the psychology of attachment and loss, why are cognitive neuroscientists not focusing their attention on the mammalian brain systems that evolved specifically for the purpose of mediating attachment and loss, and which produce the particular type of pain associated with these biological phenomena of universal significance, namely separation distress (also known as 'protest' or 'panic') which, if it does not result in reunion, is typically followed by hopeless 'despair'?
>
> It is well established that a specific mammalian brain system evolved precisely to generate these depression-like feelings....his brain system evolved from general pain mechanisms, millions of years ago, apparently for the purpose of forging long-term attachments between mothers and their offspring, between sexual mates, and ultimately between social groups in general. When such social bonds are broken through separation or loss of a loved one, or the like, then these brain mechanisms make the sufferer feel bad in a particular way. This special type of pain is called separation distress or panic. The biological value of this type of pain is that it motivates the sufferer to avoid separation, and to seek reunion with the lost object.
>
> (Solms, 2022, p 152)

The depressive reactions probably had other evolutionary advantages as well, e.g. it protected the inferior animal from further injury in fights for rank in a group of chimpanzees. One of these survival advantages seems particularly interesting for the topic here: if a primate young loses its mother, it first reacts with panic, desperate screaming and crying in order to lure the mother back to it. If this is unsuccessful within a relatively short time, a young primate is more likely to survive if it shows a kind of depressive reaction with "depressive, quiet emotions," that is, goes into a state of shock, falls silent and hides in the place where it lost its mother in order to avoid attracting predators by crying loudly, etc. This is to avoid attracting predators that find it helpless prey (see also Solms & Panksepp, 2010).

Depression can, therefore, indeed be seen as an evolutionary-biological survival mechanism as a reaction to the loss of the primate object. *For the primate young (and also for the human baby), this loss is associated with an existential, traumatic experience of total dependence, helplessness and a flood of fear of death and panic.* At the core of the traumatic experience is the experience that the self has no possibility of bringing the mother back; on the contrary, passive, "silent," "apathetic" behavior, resigned, apathetic withdrawal proves to be the best survival strategy. We have observed similar behavior in many of our chronically depressed patients: they were unconsciously deeply convinced that they could do nothing to regain the lost object, a lost state of happiness, a self-ideal, etc. They, therefore, remained in a state of apathy. They, therefore, remained in a kind of psychological state of shock, a social death reflex, a complete social withdrawal and the fantasy that the other (the primary object, the partner, the analyst) was solely responsible for freeing the self from this state. As discussed in the manual on chronic depression, this leads to important treatment considerations in order to help the patient emerge from the state of shock and resigned paralysis, to be able to mourn the traumatic loss and to regain their own mental activity (see Leuzinger-Bohleber, Fischmann & Beutel, 2022).

b) The extensive, more recent research in the field of *genetics and epigenetics is* interesting for the question of the early roots of depression and its transgenerational transmission. Salazar and Zambrano (2021) describe that there are now many studies by large research groups with several thousand patients with major depression, as well as twin and family studies, which show that the genetic component in depression is around 31–42%. Apparently, many genes play a role in this, and not just a single one, as was assumed a few years ago. These researchers currently speak of 102 different independent gene variants that are associated with depression. It is, therefore, now assumed that at least a third of our depressive patients have a genetic predisposition.

At the same time, however, many studies from the field of epigenetics show—at least to some extent—that the genetic risk only comes into play in such a predisposition if corresponding environmental stresses and, in particular, early traumatization trigger the corresponding genes. According to Jiménez and Quevedo (in print), adverse childhood experiences related to abuse (Abuse-related Adverse Childhood Experience (ACE)) are responsible for 54% of the population suffering from depression, 67% of those who attempt suicide and 64% of those who develop severe drug addiction. People who are exposed to six or more such ACEs die on average 20 years earlier. Lippard and Nemeroff (2020) also write in a recently published paper:

> Childhood maltreatment increases risk for mood disorders and is associated with earlier onset—and more pernicious disease course following onset—of mood disorders. While the majority of studies to date have been cross-sectional, longitudinal studies are emerging and support the devastating role(s) childhood maltreatment has on development of, and illness course in, mood disorders…
>
> Overwhelming evidence has accrued indicating that childhood maltreatment is associated with increased risk for, earlier age of onset, worse illness course and treatment response in MDD and bipolar disorder.
>
> (Lippard & Nemeroff, 2020, p. 25)

Right away, these findings are highly relevant for all forms of early prevention, as will shortly be discussed in our conclusion (Chapter 7). However, they are also interesting for comparative psychotherapy research and the question of structural change (see Section 1.5). Jiménez and Quevedo (in print) write in their overview article:

> Psychotherapy can modify the configuration of neural systems of emotional regulation, social cognition, and impulsivity, changing both brain activity and structure. Reprogramming gene expression of molecules attached to key biological systems of neurotransmission,

neuromodulation, neuroplasticity, and stress response. Psychotherapy can be understood as a disrupter of the 'external social recursion' that goes from the social environment to neural systems, modifying the subjective perception of the interpersonal environment, and capable of informing and changing the 'internal physiologic recursion' that ranges from the Central Nervous System to gene expression, including hormonal systems, inflammatory molecules, and intracellular signal transduction (Slavich and Cole, 2013).

(Jiménez & Quevedo, in print, manuscript p. 10)

The authors rely on relatively few studies to date and emphasize that a great deal of research, especially many long-term studies, is still needed to provide further empirical support for their view. However, they are optimistic, that future research will provide further arguments to convince health insurance companies that psychoanalysis and long-term psychoanalytic treatments, which at first glance appear to be costly in terms of time and money, are worthwhile in the long term for chronically depressed patients because they promise a lasting improvement in the psychological and psychosocial situation for those affected and their families, as well as mitigating the transgenerational transmission of their depression and traumatization. Put simply, in the sense of epigenetic research, the intensive relationship experiences with the analyst are suitable for making depressive reactions (including those caused by a genetic disposition triggered by pathological object relationships) comprehensible to the analysand, as well as for contrasting them with new, alternative relationship experiences in the transference relationship with the analyst, in the best case a central prerequisite for being able to then shape his current love and work relationships—and his generativity—in a nondepressive modality.

References

Jiménez, J. P., & Quevedo, Y. (in print). Kandel's footsteps. Epigenetic and therapeutic chance. In S. Gullestad, E. Stänicke & M. Leuzinger-Bohleber (Eds.), *Psychoanalytic Studies of Change: An Integrative Perspective*. London: Routledge.

Jiménez, J. P., Botto, A., & Fonagy, P. (2021). *Depression and Personality. Etiopathogenic Theories and Models in Depression*. Switzerland: Springer Nature.

Leuzinger-Bohleber, M., Fischmann, T., & Beutel, M. (2022). *Chronische De-pression. Psychoanalytische Langzeittherapie.* Reihe: Praxis der psychody-namischen Psychotherapie—analytische und tiefenpsychologisch fundierte Psychotherapie, Bd. 12. Göttingen: Hogrefe Verlag.

Lippard, E. T. C., & Nemeroff, C. B. (2020). The devastating clinical conse-quences of child abuse and neglect: Increased disease vulnerability and poor treatment response in mood disorders. *The American Journal of Psychiatry, 177,* 20–36. https://doi.org/10.1176/appi.ajp.2019.19010020

Panksepp, J. (2004). *Affective Neuroscience: The Foundations of Human and Animal Emotions.* New York: Oxford University Press.

Salazar, L. A., & Zambrano, T. (2021). Genetic and epigenetic determinants of depression. From basic research to translational medicine. In J. P. Jiménez, A. Botto & P. Fonagy (Eds.), *Depression and Personality. Etiopathogenic Theories and Models in Depression* (pp. 141–155). Switzerland: Springer Nature.

Solms, M. (2022). Depression in neuropsychoanalysis: Why does depression feels bad? In M. Leuzinger-Bohleber, G. Ambresin, T. Fischmann & M. Solms (Eds.), *On the Dark Side of Chronic Depression. Psychoanalytic, Social-Cultural and Research Approaches* (pp. 144–155). London: Routledge.

Solms, M., & Panksepp, J. (2010). Why depression feels bad. In E. K. Perry, D. Collerton, F. E. N. LeBeau, & H. Ashton (Eds.), *New Horizons in the Neu-roscience of Consciousness* (pp. 169–178). Amsterdam/Philadelphia: John Benjamins Publishing Company. https://doi.org/10.1075/aicr.79.23sol

Chapter 7

Summary and outlook

Let me summarize the main theses of this introductory psychoanalytic perspective on depression:

1. Empirical as well as clinical and conceptual research in psychoanalysis and evolutionary biological considerations have shown that *the central feeling of powerlessness and helplessness is at the center of depression in our times* and overlaps the pathological processing of experiences of loss in melancholy postulated by Freud or Ehrenberg's understanding of depression as a tragedy of inadequacy. From a psychoanalytical perspective, we are concerned in this context with the current social danger that populists, fundamentalists, and nationalist leaders worldwide know how to mobilize an omnipotent defense against the intolerability of depressive and traumatic feelings of powerlessness and helplessness as well as the associated unconscious fantasies and abuse them for their own purposes.

2. *Depression is a heterogeneous and complex phenomenon that requires multifactorial explanatory models*, whereby the transition from "normal," even productive depressive reactions, to the most severe forms of mental illness is fluid. Even *mild forms of depression should be taken seriously,* as first-time sufferers can usually be treated well with crisis interventions or brief therapies. At the same time, it is important to recognize the group of *15–30% of depressives who can hardly be helped with brief interventions* (cf. the meta-analyses from Falk Leichsenring's research group, among others). These are often people who have experienced severe early traumatization and already have a long history of depressive episodes behind them. They should immediately be offered more

DOI: 10.4324/9781003455349-7

intensive long-term treatment or psychoanalysis in order to spare them the frequent ordeal of many barely successful (short-term) therapies.

3. *As several studies have now shown, 70–80% of chronically depressed patients were able to achieve a lasting alleviation of their depressive symptoms in long-term psychotherapy, often in conjunction with a structural change*, that is, a lasting improvement in their quality of life, their ability to relate and work, their creativity and generativity. Moreover, for many of these traumatized, depressed people, one of the most important outcomes of therapy was that they were able to mitigate or even interrupt the passing on of depression and trauma to their children. However, several large psychoanalytical depression studies (LAC, MELAS, MODE), which are still ongoing, are investigating in more detail *which patients* with *which type of depression, in which circumstances,* benefit best from *which treatment.* This also includes the ethically and scientifically important question of which depressive patients are more likely to benefit from a non-psychoanalytical procedure.

4. Brain anatomical and physiological changes are highly likely to occur in parallel with psychological and psychosocial transformations. Various international psychoanalytic research groups are investigating this research topic (e.g. in London, Innsbruck, Zurich, Oslo, Helsinki, Stockholm, Vienna, Munich and in several centers in Germany, Switzerland and the USA in the MODE project etc.). In addition, ongoing studies are empirically studying once more that long-term psychoanalytic treatments are economically worthwhile, because successful psychoanalyses lead, among other things, to patients having fewer days of absence from work, inpatient stays, early retirement, etc. Finally, there are challenging and controversial debates on the effects of antidepressants, their mechanisms of action, indications and contraindications for combination treatments. There is still much to be done in psychoanalytic depression research!

5. *Conceptually, modern psychoanalysis* (based on Hugo Bleichmar, among others) *postulates that there are various psychodynamic pathways that lead to severe depression.* Depending on which of these pathways dominates in a particular patient, we speak of guilt depression, narcissistic depression, psychotic depression or depression that is predominantly caused by traumatization. In a flexible psychoanalytic treatment technique, both these diagnostic groups

and the idiosyncratic characteristics of each depressed individual are taken into account.

6. *Currently, a genetic predisposition of 31–42% is assumed for major depression.* However, *epigenetic research* shows that the genetic risk of such a predisposition only comes into play if the corresponding environmental stresses and, in particular, early traumatization (e.g. experiences of violence within the family or sexual abuse) trigger the corresponding genes (see, e.g. Jiménez, Botto & Fonagy, 2021). For me, this shows impressively how much we assume today that genetics *and* environment, biology *and* culture, drive *and* trauma (Grubrich-Simitis, 1979) are not opposites, but always interact in a complex way.

Thus, the central experience of powerlessness and helplessness in depressed and traumatized people focused on in this volume is usually caused simultaneously by the current personal, institutional and/or social situation, as well as by embodied memories of *primary traumatization according to Winnicott* (cf. Abram, 2021), which—from an anthropological and evolutionary-biological perspective—we have all experienced as psychophysiological premature births, albeit to varying degrees. From this knowledge derives *one* possible contribution of psychoanalysis to "dark enlightenment" (Whitebook, 2017), because neither writers[1] nor psychoanalysts can prevent wars and social catastrophes and the associated transgenerational traumatization, they can only document their consequences and bring them up in critical social debates, thereby contributing to sensitization, which in psychoanalytic treatment can at best support a healing process in the individual. In relation to the psychoanalytical depression research presented here, I would therefore like to summarize it in a somewhat bold, simplified and exaggerated way: If "good enough" object-relations experiences in the biologically determined, extremely vulnerable period of the first months and years of life enable us to develop a basic epistemic trust (Fonagy), we can psychologically endure the actualization of basic human experiences of powerlessness and dependence on others in the present, including confrontation with individual and collective traumatization, and connect them internally with the unconscious memory of experiences that there is always someone who is empathetically available to help us in this situation. This enables us to dispense with an omnipotent defense against the unbearable powerlessness and instead to react in an "adequate" depressive manner, that is, to pause, reflect and look for room for maneuvering together with others.—If, on the other hand, our early object relationships were not in a "good enough" way capable of dealing with powerlessness, panic, and fear of death, we lack such basic trust in a helping Other and the possibility of the self to actively defend itself: the basic feeling of self-agency has collapsed. It is highly likely that, like Mr A and many patients in our studies, we are then flooded internally with embodied memories of early traumatization and the experience of total loneliness and helplessness in current powerlessness situations. This usually leads to a severe depressive breakdown, a state of psychological shock, social withdrawal, passive self-destructive resignation, or even an omnipotent defense.

7. As discussed in this volume, psychoanalytic trauma research shows that—even in individuals who were lucky enough to develop a "good enough" basic trust in their first years of life—extreme traumatization, e.g. through torture, flight, and other war experiences, as well as traumatic physical experiences (e.g. polio, serious accidents, early separation trauma due to long stays in hospital, etc.) can cause the basic trust in a helping other and self-agency to collapse, with serious short-term and long-term consequences. A number of detailed case studies illustrated in this volume that such traumatization often unconsciously determines people's thoughts, feelings, and actions and is also passed on to the next generation. As the large empirical psychotherapy studies cited have shown, chronic depression is often one of the possible consequences of such severe traumatic experiences.

    As already mentioned above, many former psychoanalysis patients have described that one of the most important outcomes of their therapy was that they were able to cut the unconscious umbilical cord between the generations and no longer had to pass on their own traumatization unbroken to their children and grandchildren.

8. One conclusion from all these studies as well as from clinical psychoanalytic practice therefore seems obvious: early prevention in the sense of a "caring culture" for the next generation (Sally Weintrobe, 2013) has become an important task for our Western democracies particularly in times of war and societal catastrophies, flight, and migration connected with collective trauma.

    However, even non-traumatized nuclear families are often structurally overwhelmed in the first weeks of their babies' lives, as the family, institutional, and social networks with their important holding and containing functions have usually collapsed.

This harbors the risk that the parents, or the early central caregivers, will not be able to deal with the outlined primary traumatization (Winnicott) of their baby in a "good enough" way but may even reinforce it. This increases the likelihood of their child suffering from depression later on. Against this backdrop, the African proverb seems both wise and topical: "It takes a whole village to raise a child." The structural overload in marginalized social groups, for single parents and for (traumatized) migrants and refugees is even more dramatic. Therefore, everything possible should be done to support parents and their children in the first vulnerable years of life, personally, professionally, institutionally, financially, and through media and social education.

With this in mind, we have endeavored to make a local contribution to a caring culture for the next generation with a so-called "outreach psychoanalysis"[2] in Frankfurt a.M. We tried to bring our specific psychoanalytical knowledge of unconscious sources of difficult parenting out of the professional ivory tower into the Frankfurt community and make it available to migrants, refugees and families living on the margins of our society.

These psychoanalytical prevention projects cannot be described within the scope of this book (see e.g. Emde & Leuzinger-Bohleber, 2014; Leuzinger-Bohleber & Plänkers, 2019). However, just a short illustration of the basic idea of all these projects: The STARTHILFE project was carried out jointly by the Sigmund-Freud-Institute (SFI), a psychoanalytic research institute in Frankfurt a.M. and the Anna Freud Institut (AFI), a training institute für child and adolescent psychoanalytic psychotherapies. Following a scientific evaluation of the first results of the STARTHILFE project, the project was financially supported by the City of Frankfurt and is now in its 16th year. In the meantime, most of the 143 municipal kindergartens have implemented the project at least once in their facilities. This means that the team is offered a two-hour psychoanalytical supervision session every 14 days. Often, even psychotherapies for children at risk and their families can be discussed and initiated by the supervision. Additionally, a training candidate visits the institution one afternoon each week and supports the team. His or her psychoanalytically trained observations are discussed with the team on site.

STARTHILFE fulfills the intention of "outreach psychoanalysis" in the best sense of the word. Through its continuous implementation, STARTHILFE has reached several hundred children-at-risk and their families who live on the outskirts of our city and would hardly have found their way to a psychoanalytic outpatient clinic or a private analytic practice. In many detailed cases as well as some group statistical studies, we were able to show that many children were helped to develop amazingly well and did not end in any severe depressive illnesses, which for us is an example of successful psychoanalytic prevention. In addition, STARTHILFE was able to contribute to the professionalization of Kindergarten teachers and to build a network of psychoanalytical institutions in the urban community

9. However, we do not overestimate our contribution to a "caring culture," as *it is above all an enormous social and political task to develop a culture of solidarity, compassion, and care for the next generation* in times like ours, in which the gap between rich and poor in the Western societies, the privileged and those living on the margins of our society are drifting ever further apart, and powerlessness, helplessness and insecurity in the current, enormously threatening social situation due to the climate crises and the ongoing wars with their global consequences are increasing sharply.

Notes

1 The Ukraine writer, Serhij Zhadan, said in his speech on receiving the Peace Prize of the German Book Trade. "War changes our memory and fills it with extremely painful experiences, extremely deep traumas and extremely bitter conversations. You cannot erase this memory, you cannot ignore the past. From now on, it is part of you." (quoted in FAZ, 24.10.2022, p. 29).

2 At the psychoanalytic center at Myliusstr. 20 in Frankfurt, we have implemented a whole series of such early prevention projects over many

years—thanks to productive collaboration between the Sigmund-Freud-Institut (SFI), the Anna Freud Institut (AFI), the Frankfurt Psychoanalytic Institut (FPI), the Frankfurter Arbeitsgemeinschaft für Psychoanalytische Pädagogik (FAPP), the Jewish Counselling Centre, partly in close co-operation with the IDeA Centre (Individual Development and Adaptive Education of Children at Risk): the Frankfurt Prevention Study, the ADHD Effectiveness Study, the EVA studies, the FIRST Steps projects, the STARTHILFE project and finally the STEP-BY-STEP project, which is fortunately being continued by my successor at SFI, Patrick Meurs (see Emde & Leuzinger-Bohleber, 2014; Leuzinger-Bohleber & Plänkers, 2019).

References

Abram, J. (2021). On Winnicott's concept of trauma. *The International Journal of Psychoanalysis, 102*(4), 778–793.

Emde, R. N., & Leuzinger-Bohleber, M. (Eds.) (2014). *Early Parenting and Prevention of Disorder: Psychoanalytic Research at Interdisciplinary Frontiers*. London: Karnac.

Grubrich-Simitis, I. (1979). Extreme traumatization as cumulative trauma: Psychoanalytic studies of mental after-effects of concentration camp imprisonment. *Psyche—Z Psychoanal, 33*(11), 991–1023.

Jiménez, J. P., Botto, A., & Fonagy, P. (Eds.) (2021). *Etiopathogenic Theories and Models in Depression*. Cham: Springer International Publishing.

Leuzinger-Bohleber, M., & Plänkers, T. (2019). The struggle for a psychoanalytic research institute: The evolution of Frankfurts sigmund-freud-institute. *The International Journal of Psychoanalysis, 100*(5), 962–987.

Weintrobe, S. (Ed.) (2013). *Engaging With Climate Change: Psychoanalytic and Interdisciplinary Perspectives*. London: Routledge.

Whitebook, J. (2017). *Freud: An Intellectual Biography*. Cambridge: Cambridge University Press.

Index

Note: Locators followed by 'n' refer to note numbers.